BETTER YOU BETTER DOG BETTER LIFE

30 DAYS TO HAPPINESS WITH YOUR BEST FRIEND

BETTER YOU BETTER DOG BETTER LIFE

Tricia Montgomery
Dr. Ernie Ward
Dr. David Levine

copyright © 2019 Tricia Montgomery, Ernie Ward, and David Levine

Please inquire for rights, other than text for promotion, to reproduce material from this book.

Better You Better Dog Publishing
PO BOX 4945
Chattanooga, TN 37405

www. betteryoubetterdog.com.

Printed in the United States of America.

ISBN: 978-1-943661-17-6

Cover photos: Creative Commons

CONTENTS

Celebrity Foreword	ix
Foreword	xi
Introduction	1
Week One: Motivating for Positive Change	7
Week Two: Nutrition, Weight, and Optimal Health	37
Week Three: Physical Activity and Optimal Health	83
Week Four: Building Community	135
Appendices	153
References	167

DEDICATIONS

To say this has been a journey would be an understatement. Thank you to Ernie and David and all of those who committed their time, treasures and talents to share stories, wisdom and excellence. A special thanks to my Mom, my sisters, Karen and Cheryl, and Beckie Mossor, for the beautiful honesty, friendship, bond, and belief. To my daughter Gabrielle and son Jonathan, you are my heart and I am so proud of you both. To Chris Bobowski, thank you for your unwavering support and dedication. With God all things are possible.

—Tricia Montgomery

I'd like to dedicate this book to my North Star and wife for the past 33 years, Laura, our two daughters, Madison and Taylor, and the thousands of pet parents and their furry family members who have allowed me to guide them on their journey to better health and well-being over the past 27 years of veterinary practice.

—Ernie Ward

Thanks first to my co-editors and friends, Tricia and Ernie, who are not only exceptional in their fields but who are also exceptional people. To my mother Marie, to whom I owe much more than I can ever repay. To my children Lauren Allyn, Sarah Marie, Hadley Christian, and Ava Katherine Ann who brighten every moment of every day. To my wife and best friend Allison who supports me wholly in my many endeavors. And to the One who was with me before I was born.

—David Levine

FOREWORD

If you are ready to change your life, you can. I don't care how many times you have tried and failed. No matter who you are, where you are, or what you are doing, you can change your life. This book is here to help you.

The good news? We're in this together. You, me, David, and Ernie, and your beloved dog are with you every step of the way. Together, we have the ability to transform your life to be the person that you have always wanted to be, a better version of you. And you can start making this change now. All you need to do is determine what is holding you back and make new choices.

I personally transformed, not just the outside, but more importantly, the inside. I am most certainly not the person I was twenty years ago, or for that matter, one year ago. And a lesson I learned in this process was perhaps an even better lesson, unlearning something about myself. If you get into the habit of doing things the same way or fishing on the same side of the boat, things don't change. But you may say, "I'm not losing weight. I still feel tired. I'm still in a bad mood" or "I didn't catch any fish." Well, move to the other side of the boat. Try something different. Take a new approach. Take away the history and look ahead. Unlearning takes time and is a process. Change doesn't happen overnight, but your attitude certainly can.

This change is not about never making another unhealthy choice or never having another mocha latte or chocolate bar. It's about giving you the options, and the inspiration, to not be a victim. It's also about not pretending that things are fine when they really aren't. It's about you and goals that are within your reach with our best friends beside us who help us "go for the bone."

My hope for you is that you read this book and be inspired to pursue a healthier lifestyle for both you and your dog. I want you to take the time and listen with your heart, instead of the doubts and the *coulda, shoulda, woulda* folks, and challenge yourself to go into the unknown.

Everything you desire is waiting for you. Let's let the dogs out, get them moving, and get ready for your new leash on life.

—Tricia Montgomery

INTRODUCTION

On your journey to a better you, a better dog, and a better life with your best friend, you are in good company with three of the country's foremost authorities in specialties designed to bring out the best in you and your canine companion. You have their guarantee to be forthright and nonjudgmental as they prescribe for you a solid path to happiness with your best friend, your dog. The three experts you'll be working with are health and wellness specialist Tricia Montgomery; Dr. Ernie Ward, a veterinarian, canine obesity expert, author of *Chow Hounds: Why Our Dogs are Getting Fatter*, and founder of the Association for Pet Obesity Prevention; and canine and human fitness expert Dr. David Levine, author of the textbook *Canine Rehabilitation and Physical Therapy* and many other books, and professor at the University of Tennessee at Chattanooga.

As a nation, we are truly amid a crisis, an epidemic of obesity, poor fitness, and even loneliness, all of which contribute to reduced health and unhappiness. An estimated 53.8 percent of US dogs are overweight or obese; that's 41.9 million dogs [1]. More than one-third (36.5 percent) of U.S. adults are obese and two-thirds are either obese or overweight; that's 215 million citizens. And the U.S. is not alone. The obesity and overweight rate in Canada is 41 percent. In the United Kingdom, the number is even higher at 66 percent. In China, the rate is roughly 13 percent, rising to 20 percent in the cities. So, if you are overweight or obese, you are not alone.

Regarding fitness, specifically heart fitness, activities such as walking, jogging, and floor exercises that increase your heart rate and perhaps even raise a sweat are significantly linked to decreased risks for a variety of health problems, including hypertension. In one research study, improved cardio-respiratory fitness resulted in a 42 percent reduction in all causes of mortality [2]. That's huge.

And what about loneliness? According to Deborah Wells, "A substantial body of research now points to the idea that pets can reduce feelings of loneliness and isolation" [3]. Wells also finds that there is less depression among the elderly who own pets and also among persons living with life-threatening conditions who own pets [3]. Not only is social isolation a risk factor for early mortality, but also just thinking that you are alone is detrimental to your health. According to researchers, "Being socially connected is not only influential for psychological and emotional well-being but it also has a significant and positive influence on physical well-being" [4]. And what about that indicator of loneliness, depression? The CDC estimates that 8 percent of Americans suffer from moderate to severe depression, with the highest numbers (12 percent) among women aged 40–59, and that does not include the millions of people who suffer from minor depression, which can have equally bad health outcomes. And your dog, remember your dog. Dogs suffer from obesity, poor fitness, and get lonely and suffer from depression as well [5].

In 1992, 130 pounds overweight and looking for answers, Tricia Montgomery took a candid look at her life, realizing that not only was she unhealthy and unhappy, but that her beloved basset hound Louie was as well. They started off easy, walking and then graduating to climbing bleacher stairs at a nearby stadium. She didn't know it at the time, but she had begun a journey to help others regain their health and happiness in the good company of a faithful companion. Tricia knows too well the apathy and distress that one's poor health can lead to and found the motivation she needed close at hand, her dog Louie.

Better you, Better Dog, Better life

Tricia has realized her dream of not only caring for herself but also of earning the empathy needed to help others in their journey to a better life. "My dog gave me an unconditional reason to make it okay for me to exercise," says Tricia, and she sees that over and over again in her clients. Our best friends do not judge and deserve our utmost. Often, taking up a healthy lifestyle is a case of doing it for the dog. "Our best friends open the door and give us the reason to succeed," says Tricia. In Week One, "Motivating for Positive Change," you'll meet Tricia and see what she does best as she leads you through the first week of your wellness adventure with your dog at your side.

As veterinarians go, Dr. Ernie Ward breaks the mold. He truly has you and your pet's nutrition and wellness at heart. An avid endurance athlete and multiple Ironman completer, Ernie knows the value of a calorie, where it comes from, and how it will affect you and your dog. As a national advocate for pet health, Ernie specializes in making sure that his canine clients achieve healthy weights and eat nutritious foods. And he notes that better eating habits for the dog often spreads to the owner. What you don't know about your pet's dog food and the servings you provide may come as a surprise as you begin your journey to better nutrition in Week Two, "Nutrition, Weight, and Optimal Health."

Ernie is a clinician who owns a private veterinary practice and is a sought-after speaker, promoting healthy lifestyles for both pets and people. Whether you own your first puppy or you share your home with a senior dog, Ernie can tailor a specific health plan to bring out the best in you and your pet. As his website states: "Dr. Ernie has a unique talent for making the most complex and challenging concepts easy to understand and relatable."

Professor David Levine believes that any fitness plan, whether for you or your dog, should be fun, and he provides that for you in this book. Although always researching the latest fitness and rehabilitation technology, such as regenerative medicine and therapeutic lasers, David keeps his feet on the ground, bridging the gap between the world of humans and dogs. As a physical therapist who works with both people and canines, David knows the importance of taking it slow and setting goals to improve both your and your dog's fitness.

Since 1990, David has taught and researched at the University of Tennessee at Chattanooga and holds a chair of excellence within the Department of Physical Therapy. David always has fitness on his mind and an easy way of making seemingly complicated or boring fitness goals simple and fun. In Week Three, "Physical Activity and Optimal Health," you'll meet David and begin your third week's journey into fulfilling your fitness goals with your faithful canine.

Week Four, "Building Community," is a collaborative chapter with Tricia, Ernie, and David weighing in. Often on a journey to wellness and happiness, you may find yourself in a vacuum, alone to face the world and make good things happen. There may be the sense of a void, perhaps even a sadness that accompanies you on your journey, and that's where community becomes the fourth tool of success, in tandem with motivation, nutrition, and physical activity.

Making up your mind, though, to make changes for a lifestyle that promises immediate and long-term rewards is empowering and enlightening. Realizing that you have others along for the journey creates an urgency to succeed. You may even find yourself excited that you are setting out on a journey for a better you, a better dog, a better life. Why not go all the way and share your new way of life with others? We all need encouragement, including our dogs, and that's what building a community around your quest will do.

Rest assured that Tricia, Ernie, and David have your best

interest at heart. They will acccompany you for the first thirty days, and beyond, and provide you with the tools to maintain your momentum and reach health goals for you and for your dog. In addition, in Week Four, they will make specific recommendations designed to help you build that all-important web of support that will keep you on track for the months and years to come.

For more information on your personal trainers visit these websites:

Tricia Montgomery: www.betteryoubetterdog.com

Dr. Ernie Ward: www.DrErnieWard.com
and PetObesityPrevention.org

Dr. David Levine: en.wikipedia.org/wiki/David_F._Levine

For more information on this book, with additional tips for a healthy lifestyle with your dog, visit:

www.betteryoubetterdog.com.

WEEK ONE: MOTIVATING FOR POSITIVE CHANGE

—Tricia Montgomery—

Welcome! What follows is practical advice on how to get motivated for your thirty-day journey to a better you, a better dog, and a better life. Life is challenging, and we all need the most support that we can get. Some of the stories you will read involve overcoming health problems, which we all face at one time or another. We want you to be inspired by others and their struggles for better health. One of the best allies in this quest for health and happiness is your dog, your best friend. To begin, let me tell you my story. In addition to battling my weight and fitness level, I face my own unique health challenges, and I imagine, if we dig a little deeper, and listen more, you have yours as well.

In 2015, I was diagnosed with a disease related to Guillain–Barré syndrome. The disease leaves me weak and uncoordinated. What causes this disease is not yet clear. It's a one in a million diagnosis, and I was devastated. Every three weeks I undergo hospital treatments, receiving IV medications, which cause serious nausea and headaches.

An active cross-trainer and marathoner before the disorder hit, my disease has taken its toll, but has strengthened my resolve. Through the disorder I have come to realize even more that our health is precious, and that it is my calling to help others achieve a healthy lifestyle, especially in tandem with our faithful canine friends. Sitting in a hospital bed, watching the IV medicines drip into my vein, I think about all of the extraordinary people I have met, people with real problems who only need that little push, who with their pet make their lives healthy and productive. Without them, my own personal journey is less important.

I've had so much taken away from me by my disease, but my purpose in life has only been strengthened. I've had my share of pity parties, crying, and my share of self-doubt. I only want more to reach out more and touch the lives of others, you included, to bring them closer to their full potential, whether it be battling weight gain or simply opening up to a supportive social setting. To put it simply, I want to help you and your dog. Together, so much can be accomplished. My goal is to showcase for you that health is achievable, no matter the odds. I'm alive! I'm able to walk with my dog and make a point of eating nutritious foods. Life is a gift, and I want to share that with you.

Sometimes I can't feel my left leg, and sometimes holding things is a challenge. Often at meetings I feel terribly fatigued, but my family, friends, clients, and my faithful dog Zeus help me to push forward. I learned about boxing and the work aimed at stimulating my brain through high impact movements and exercises. I now box three times a week. My coordination and movements have become smoother, and I can definitely see a change in my endurance. Through boxing, I met Scott Quittschau, an amazing personal trainer and friend. Scott realized my muscles were beginning to atrophy; they were not being used. He took the time, held onto me through squats, lunges, and stairs, pushing me every step of the way as I gained strength. I also exercise every day with Zeus. So, what has this taught me? It's humbled me. How many people are afraid, how many people struggle with the seen and most importantly with the unseen? It's made me empathize with others like you who need and want to be healthy. I look at someone and think, "What are they struggling with?" So many of the stories I hear inspire me.

And, not only have I learned to listen to others through my disorder, I've become adept at listening through my work with clients. I think that people are often judgmental. Often, I meet people who feel that they have been labeled. It's easy to bottle up the negative views that others may hold toward you. But, we have touching stories to tell. We have no idea what's inside a person, and often it's my job to bring that story out, to uncover the pain, and offer hope through very practical advice.

I remember speaking to Colleen. She was very bubbly with an apple dumpling face. One day her son told her that she should be on *The Biggest Loser* TV show, devastating her, but it was true. Harsh as it was, that changed her. Although it made her sad and cry, her son's words set her on a path of self-discovery where she, like so many others, learned to make her life better through physical activity and better nutrition with her dog.

Women are more likely to be obese and suffer from depression than men, across all age groups. Most clients that I help are women, but men are vulnerable as well. Often, it's just a case of loneliness. We live in a society that can be very alienating, especially if you don't live up to society's expectations of perfect weight and fitness. In my world, a person can walk in with his or her dog and be accepted unconditionally. It's liberating to find community and to be surrounded by supportive people.

But, although loneliness is often a factor, I do find that most people's basic need is help with their weight, nutrition, and fitness. Losing weight, eating better, and increasing physical activity brings a bounty of health rewards, including increased self-esteem and a new confidence to face the world. The statistics on overweight and obesity, for both dogs and people, are alarming. An estimated 53.8 percent of U.S. dogs are overweight or obese [1]. That's 41.9 million U.S. dogs. More than one-third (36.5 percent) of U.S. adults are obese [6]. That's 112 million who are obese, and 215 million who are overweight. Financially, the medical costs of an obese person average $1,500 more per year than non-obese people, so there are many reasons why pets and people can benefit from weight loss.

But, it's important not to blame yourself. Life happens, the weight accumulates, and it can be very disheartening. My clients will come in with an obese dog, stating that they're there for the dog, but it's the person who is seeking help, and that's okay. I'm never there to judge, but to be supportive. The more I listen, the more the person talks. I see a smile. I see a tail wag, and know that I'm making a difference, that there is hope for us all. And now for our first story. Like me, Mary has had to overcome a major health problem, in her case an injury, finding the inspiration she needs from her dogs, friends, and family.

MARY'S STORY

Following a horrific head injury, which left her disabled, Mary is all about building community for dogs and their owners. Mary is the most loving and caring person you will ever meet. As an example, Mary is an American Red Cross Pet CPR/First Aid Instructor, having dedicated her life to health and healing in the canine community. Although thoroughly into dogs now, Mary began her animal career working with horses.

Sadly, Mary's work with horses came to a sudden and tragic end. This is how she tells the story:

I was just short of my thirtieth birthday in 1988. I was a very independent woman up to the time of the accident, working with horses and handicapped persons, rehabilitating them through equine (horse) therapy.

I was raising yearlings, and we were at the phase where we were mounting the horses while being led by a groundsman. I rode out of the barn onto very thick sand, which keeps the horse from picking up speed and prevents injury if the horse gets rowdy. Suddenly, the horse startled, and she reared up. I held on for dear life, but instead of allowing her to go forward, the groundsman pushed back on the horse's head and over I went backwards with the horse on top of us, breaking the groundsman's legs. I was terrified. Everyone came running. I rolled onto my belly, still conscious. Then, the horse raced back toward me and went to jump but placed her full weight on my head. I was immediately knocked out and stopped breathing. Although the horse was okay and went on to a racing career, I was declared dead at the scene, but luckily revived through CPR.

At first the doctors didn't think I would make it. From my head injury, there was tremendous brain swelling. It took weeks to recover, and at first I could not walk or even chew and underwent intense physical therapy. I began a process, learning how to compensate for the areas damaged, but lapsed into a deep depression, and ultimately my first marriage failed. I'm now at a place where it's mainly the physical impairments that slow me down, and I still have a terrible time with short-term memory. I'm definitely different after the accident, but even more committed to helping others with disability, especially through canine therapy, the one thing that has brought me back to the land of the living.

So, no pity required here. I did eventually re-marry and have been married to a wonderful man, Mark, for eighteen years. Although we have struggled financially, the biggest downside to my injury was social rejection, not being able to contribute to my community and family. Persons with disabilities often don't get the respect they deserve and are often overlooked, but that drove me forward to make a difference. By helping others, I help myself. One of my first success stories was with a young man, Kyle, who was in his early twenties. He couldn't afford the extra therapy he needed, so I took him on at no charge. He wore braces on his legs as a result of a childhood illness and was very quiet, almost nonverbal.

What opened the door to Kyle was the therapy dog, Jessie. Kyle wanted so much to speak to that dog. The dog was in therapy as well with a seizure disorder. I put them side-by-side on a treadmill, and Kyle would get this amazing smile. He would forget that he was exercising! He was doing it for the dog. They were helping each other. I too was still struggling with my own difficulties walking but working with people like Kyle allowed me to be me, to pay it forward, to slow down, and to use my gifts.

Even though my story began with horses, I've always had dogs. My first dog was a seven-year-old Chinese pug who lived until she was twenty-one. I'd always enjoyed working with dogs and people, but my injury really showed me what I could do with that energy. Since the accident, my canine friends have helped me in so many ways, including my depression, which lingers still. Dogs are my best friends, give me emotional support, and the will to take a simple walk. I was so active before the accident and like Kyle I had to start off slowly, walking on a treadmill. It was my dog Sarge who became my best friend and best workout partner. Two words: unconditional love.

I have five dogs now, but it was my boxer Sarge who brought me back to life, helping me to be more independent. He is able to fetch a bottle of water if I need it. There are often times when my vision is blurry or I see double If my vision goes, but Sarge can find the door for me. On his own he alerts me. He signals me with barks if he thinks I am about to fall. With my other dogs, Sarge keeps me engaged. I truly believe that I will live longer because of them. Sarge is still with me and helps me with clients as well.

Sarge was found at twelve weeks old. I was teaching at the time. There was a terrible snowstorm, only two blocks from my business. We got a call that a dog needed rescuing and my husband found this puppy that was nearly frozen. That was on December 9, what we now call Sarge's birthday. He was skinny and wormy but had a real heart of gold. Unlike most boxers, he still has his tail, which whips back and forth. He's a unique friend and dog. My newest dog is Spirit, a white boxer that was born deaf. She has developed a keen awareness of nonverbal communication, understands simple sign language, and has really enjoys working out with clients. Sometimes she just follows me like a baby duck.

Looking back, I've learned a lot since my accident. I really had to focus on how I could help myself and then begin to transfer that desire to be well with others. I recognized my talent, overcame health and weight obstacles, and put myself to work helping others through canine therapy. I still have problems, such as my short-term memory, and I limp. I still can't drive. But whereas I lost many years to my accident, I have now gained them back through my love of dogs and helping others. Just to be able to contribute again is a true gift. The simple act of taking Sarge to a women's homeless shelter lets me know that I was meant to survive. My dogs have brought me back to a safe and nurturing place. I hope that my story inspires you to overcome the barriers that may be preventing you from living life to its fullest.

HAPPINESS WITH YOUR DOG

Often, whether looking to lose weight or to be more physically active, it's a matter of achieving happiness, and what better way to do that than with your dog? We may not admit it, but unhappiness is widespread and due to many factors, including genetics and the stresses of life. Being overweight, from my own personal experience, is depressing for both dogs and people. Dogs seem to enrich our lives through a variety of mechanisms. It's been reported that blood pressure decreases in the presence of dogs. The physical and emotional contact reduces stress. People confide in their pets, sharing their deepest concerns. There is a real intimacy that is formed. There is also a uniquely physical component of the dog-human bond. We co-evolved with the dog, first trekking, hunting, and gathering together. There is a physical and biological need to walk the dog that satisfies something ancient within us. However, times have changed. We've become more sedentary. We sit in chairs. We no longer hunt for food but go to restaurants and the grocery store. Unfortunately, the way we've domesticated dogs, we wind up not getting much out of the deal. Although dogs are bred now primarily for companionship, we don't take advantage of those needs that enrich us physically and psychologically.

Being unhappy is devastating. The three primary indicators of happiness are "social support, incomes and healthy life expectancy" [7]. More than one out of twenty Americans twelve years of age and older (7.6 percent) have reported current depression. The most depression, 12 percent, is found in women aged forty to fifty-nine [8]. So, in this land of plenty, there are many who find lack of meaning, who feel unhappy or depressed. Having a healthy mental outlook on life can often be achieved through the four things: motivation, good nutrition, fitness, and community. Those four things are very important to achieve, both for you and your dog. When a dog loses weight, he becomes more animated, more energetic, and that's true of people too. While you're getting fit through good nutrition and physical activity with your dog, you begin to feel better, more alive.

And I think that happiness follows. Of course, serious depression is perhaps beyond just weight loss and fitness. That's why there is Prozac and psychotherapy. I am not a physician and do not pretend to be able to cure depression, but I am here to open up the possibility of greater happiness with your dog, which is defined by a basic sense of peace. I think happiness can be sitting with someone or just gazing at a tree on a sunny day. Happiness comes in so many different forms. There is a real need to be happy. With your dog providing confidence and security, you can work on a better you, a better dog, a better life. That's what it's all about. Now, I would like to share Peter's story.

PETER'S STORY

Peter was severely depressed and had lost the will to live. But first, before I let Peter tell his story, let me caution you, if you feel this way you should immediately seek medical attention. Do not wait to see if a dog will help you like it did Peter. The number for the National Suicide Prevention Lifeline is 1-800-273-8255. And so, here is Peter's inspirational story.

I was hesitant to tell this story but there are many people out there who need motivation to live a full life, and I want to help, just as I have been helped. It's only fair, right? Why spend life being unhappy and depressed.

In my teens, I noticed that life was difficult. I had no motivation to exercise, eat healthy, or take care of myself. I was not part of the popular crowd at school and only had one or two casual friends, no one that I could really count on. As the years passed, I became more withdrawn and occasionally had thoughts of hurting myself. I was thirty pounds overweight and lived on a diet of junk food. I sometimes just felt bad that I was alive, that I didn't deserve to be happy.

My parents, I think, were at a loss over what to do. The word depression was never spoken as if it did not exist. To be honest, even I never considered that I was depressed, although I knew that I was unhealthy. I just figured that I was second-best and that whatever I was suffering was deserved as a result. With my entry into college at Ohio State in 1981, my spirits lifted as I began to explore the world on my own terms. But soon, by my junior year, the self-hatred was back in full force, following a breakup with a girl that I loved. After that, I kind of just drifted into this shallow ditch that seemed to be filled with mud that I would trudge through day after day, oblivious to the fullness of life that I was missing.

I managed to graduate. In hindsight this seems like a major miracle, considering that I missed classes on occasion. I then found an okay job working at a large insurance firm, sitting alone in my cubicle day after day, reviewing claims. I suppose the job suited me in some ways, enabling my desire to be alone.

Gradually, partly through my job reviewing claims, and then through some research on my own, I began to put the pieces together and realized that I was depressed. It was kind of like a bell went off in my head. Prozac was still five years away, but I felt empowered by my own self-diagnosis, even without treatment, which seemed to me a drastic measure.

My life dragged along, always with that blah feeling. I ate badly and never exercised. I would work and go home and sleep. Sleep was my one and only joy. I tried to date on occasion, but usually could not get up the nerve to ask anyone out.

And then the bottom dropped out. I won't bother you with the details, but I truly wanted to die and found myself in a doctor's office, sobbing and heaving for the first time in a long while. My doctor was patient and not surprisingly diagnosed me with depression and prescribed an antidepressant. Although he didn't mention better eating habits, he did recommend that I be more physically active.

It took a while, but I noticed improvement, and was soon back on my feet, having missed two weeks of work. At one of my doctor's visits, the doctor (his name was Hal) suggested something that I thought was extremely odd. He suggested I get a pet, something to take care of and worry about. Those were his words. It took me a week or so to think about it, and I remembered the little poodle that my parents had when I was just a kid. I had really liked that dog, but she had been hit a by a car and was just suddenly gone. I don't think I realized how hurt I was at the time of her passing.

Zoos depress me, reminding me of how I felt caged, and I thought it would be the same way with the local dog shelter. But as soon as I heard (and smelled) all of those dogs filled with life and a longing just to be loved I really felt my heart lift. It was an Aha moment. Just like Dr. Hal had said, I needed something to love, to take care of. What I wasn't expecting was all of the love that I would receive back.

I have to admit, Lucy chose me. She was a pug-nosed bulldog with a little stubby tail that wagged when I leaned over to pet her. She had the deepest brown eyes and snuffled instead of breathed. I always thought that dogs from the shelter were skinny and mangy, but Lucy was nicely fat with smooth white and brown fur.

When I brought Lucy home, I had no idea what to do with her. Years later, when I had my first child, it was the same feeling. Of course, I went to the pet store and bought Lucy the best food, a red collar with a matching leash, and a big bag of doggie treats. There was a kid's book on how to take care of your dog, and I bought that too.

Finally, I had a real reason to get up in the morning! Lucy slept on my bed from day one and would start moving around before my alarm went off. I couldn't wait to get her out of the house and go on one of our walks through a neighborhood that I had never really paid attention to or appreciated very much. It was like a whole new world had opened up for me. While I was at work, I would think about our walk when I got home. For the first time, I was genuinely happy and felt that I had a real reason for living. Not only did I feel better, I also lost weight, about fifteen pounds. So, take heart and realize that a dog can be your best friend and motivate you for positive change.

THE SOCIAL SUPPORT NETWORK

Another way I like to look at enhancing life is through building one's social support network. Working together, we have a family. We are family. You, me, Ernie, and David. Often all that is needed is a text or a hug. As I often say, you never know someone's situation until you walk in their shoes. The levels of personal pain and hurt out there can be overwhelming and to overcome that often requires the help of others. There is a blame game that some people play with themselves. Put that blame aside and take charge of your life. You have your dog right there by your side, along for a journey that may at first be intimidating, but one that is richly rewarding. You have to accept you for you, aside from what family or friends may think. I have a friend whose dad used to comment when passing a truck stop that he should stop and weigh her. That thought has plagued her, but she's risen above that and is now on a personal journey to better health despite what others may think.

Better you, Better Dog, Better life

There is no need to fear that you have to become an Olympic runner or yoga expert to achieve your goals. There is a reasonable balance between good nutrition, physical activity, and maintaining a healthy weight. Everyone is different and moves forward at a different speed. It's just important that you find your own comfort zone and that you move at your own pace, surrounding yourself with people who want the best for you. This book will take you through a thirty-day journey to find that balance, to get you going on an ideal path of health and well-being with your dog. You want to achieve health, fitness, and wellness at both ends of the leash. We are here for you, as well as your dog. We are your first step at gaining a community of support.

You'll find that your dog provides motivation to create a better self. You see your dog losing weight, and it creates hope. You see your dog more active, and it creates energy. Your dog allows you to have an unconditional reason to make it okay for you to engage in healthy eating and physical activity. You will experience that dog-human bond. You are doing something good for you and something good for your pet. It's easy to give your dog a treat but spending time with your dog working up a sweat is special.

Let me tell you about my dog Louie, a basset hound, who is no longer with me, but who inspired my own personal journey to wellness. I was obese and so was he. What had happened to me had happened to my dog. We just began walking and doing things together. There was a local school stadium, and I began walking the bleacher stairs with him. With Louie by my side, eating better along with exercise became a habit. This fueled my desire to help people to love their dogs and achieve better health together. I had an opportunity to become Public Education Director of the Chicago Veterinary Medical Association, and then went on to become the Executive Director.

Through the veterinary profession and amazing veterinarians, with their knowledge of healthy living, I saw the light. Poor health runs up and down the leash. As we become more unhealthy, so do our dogs.

Now I have Zeus to keep me motivated. Zeus is a red-nosed pit bull. He is my heart and soul. A rescue dog, he was skittish, especially around other dogs. But he has helped me to continue my journey for better health, and I couldn't do it without him. On an average day, he goes everywhere with me, even to the beauty salon. He loves to go see the residents where my Mom lives and has a smile and wag for all. We walk for a mile and a half in the morning, with three half-mile walks throughout the day when possible. I also have exercise equipment in the house, which we enjoy together. He truly is my best friend.

In Week Four—Building Community, we will go into more depth on how to acquire a community of people who help to motivate you. A first step, though, is to find that special canine companion, if you do not already have one. Then, it's a matter of getting out of the house and exploring your social support network with your best friend, who will surprisingly bring you into closer contact with others who have your best interest at heart.

FEELING BETTER WITH YOUR BEST FRIEND

First, you have to accept yourself, no matter where you may be with your weight or where your dog's weight may be. This is key. We are not here to blame ourselves for being overweight or obese. Life is complicated and often results in unhealthy outcomes. It happens. Also, it may simply be a matter of getting older and perhaps letting yourself go. We change and adapt, doing the best that we can. Your body goes to a place that mirrors your overall life. Being a reader of this book, though, indicates a willingness or need to try something that is perhaps new or different. I want to motivate you and get you thinking in this first week of your journey of the key ways for you to be healthier and happier with a healthier and happier dog.

The four keys to achieving happiness with your best friend are motivation, nutrition (notice I didn't say diet), physical activity, and community. For now, I, Ernie, and David are your community. We're your cheerleaders. But ultimately you want to reach out to those who can help you in your journey to happiness.

I'm here to motivate you to grab that golden ring, to support you as Ernie guides you to proper nutrition and David coaches you to a level of activity that supports your health goals. Then, at the end of this book, we'll send you on a journey to acquire that community that is so important to maintain one's newfound health and happiness. So, let's talk about nutrition briefly.

The research is clear. We're finding out more and more that being overweight or obese leads to many other health problems. Perhaps you are overweight and suffer from high blood pressure or other diseases caused by obesity or overweight. Controlling your weight under those circumstances becomes doubly important to your health. Perhaps you have sore knees or ankles, and you find walking uncomfortable or painful. Losing excess pounds will relieve a lot of the stress that is being put on your joints. Even losing just five pounds can make a big difference each time you take a step.

Eating healthy and engaging in physical activity will point your body in the right direction. Your body will go to a weight that it's meant to be at. But, it's not without effort, and that's what makes doing this journey with your dog so important. As you see your dog's health and happiness improve, it will motivate you to keep at it for yourself. As we may say more than once in this book, health and wellness occur at both ends of the leash. You will have an unconditional reason to succeed. Your dog will encourage you to eat more nutritious foods. Your dog will make it okay for you to walk or even jog. At first, eating healthy and training with your dog may just be an excuse, but over time a better diet and physical activity will become integral to how you view the world and structure your day. It's easy to give your dog a treat, but spending time with your dog is special, and you'll both benefit.

Recently, while undergoing treatment for my disorder, I had a couple of setbacks, the paralysis in my limbs returning. I'm determined not to let my spirit slip, although it can be tempting. Luckily, I have my faithful Zeus to keep me in balance. I drive myself pretty hard, so need my time with Zeus to relax and just feel better. Sometimes I feel like one of those Bozo punching bags. I get knocked back, but my healthy habits bring me right back up. Sometimes it's tempting to just run through a fast-food joint and grab a hamburger, but I think about Zeus and draw comfort from him. He's depending on me to be healthy and happy, and I can't let him down. Life is full of hard knocks, and it's important to have a steady base from which to spring back. I had a friend recently who had been diagnosed with breast cancer. Still, she exercised with her dog. Her foends and family gathered around her, lending her support, lending her dog support. Your dog is always going to be there for you no matter what. There will also be others in your community who can be supportive, so seek them out boldly and take heart.

One question I'm often asked is how I manage my extensive travel and making sure that Zeus still gets his exercise. In Week Four, we'll discuss the all-important development of a community around you that helps you achieve your goals. One aspect of community, in regard to travel, is having those you trust to take care of your dog while you are away. Through my work with fellow dog lovers, I have found an incredible group of dog sitters who stay the night with Zeus. My sitters truly care about and love Zeus, and I often receive texts with pictures of Zeus out on his walk. So, start to think about your journey not only as a journey to health and wellness, but also one that builds relationships and friends. Initially you may be alone, but a community that helps you reach your goals is a key to success.

WHAT INSPIRES ME?

I'm lucky that I had great parents. They still inspire me to this day. Even though my dad has passed away, my mom carries me through with support and unconditional love. They always wanted what was best for me, so I was lucky. Celebrities that I admire include Ellen DeGeneres and Oprah Winfrey. They do incredible work for others, but so do my friends, like Kelly and Christine, who have been through many challenges. They have found the way over the hurdles and have come out better and stronger on the other side. I keep going back to this idea of getting to know people, and that's so important. You have to understand people, what they've been through, what they're up against. It's my passion to motivate and inspire others, but I have to put in some research and watch and listen to the stories that make up a person.

I like to talk about my step-son Jonathan, who has battled with his weight since childhood. You'll get a full account of his story in just a minute. He had been on a good path, but a divorce and depression took over and the weight started to come back as he "let himself go." When he was a kid, I would have to lock up the flour and sugar because he would find a way to make it taste good and eat it straight from the bag. During this time, he hit 300 pounds but reached back to lessons he'd learned at what some would call a "fat camp" and now is back in control. He's an incredible, loving, and giving person and is someone I admire and am continually inspired by.

We hear that same old story of gaining and losing weight, the yo-yo that seems never ending—I've been there many times. Like my son, I would find myself approaching 300 pounds and feel hopeless. It was that dog of mine, good old Louie who gave me the courage to get out of the house and exercise. I was still into the dieting mindset, but as I progressed physically and mentally, my nutrition shifted as well, away from the comfort of fast food and toward healthy choices like salads, vegetables, and lean meat. Let's just say that obesity runs in the family.

So, I'll let Jonathan tell you his story. I think my years of watching him struggle with his weight gave me insight into my own unhealthy condition. Disclaimer—although we had a dog, this story doesn't specifically involve a dog, just Jonathan and his story.

JONATHAN'S STORY

I wasn't always overweight, but the weight started to pile on around fourth grade. My parents divorced around that time with my dad moving out. It was then that I developed some unhealthy habits. My mom noticed, of course, and she began to hide the goodies from me, but I was an expert at sniffing out their location. It's hard to describe, but I felt a sense of deprivation. I wouldn't eat just one granola bar…I would eat ten. Throughout middle school, I became noticeably heavy. Since I had been a little kid, hockey was my favorite sport, but as I put on the pounds I became less confident on the ice and finally dropped out in sixth grade. I just couldn't keep up. And so, in addition to eating and eating, I exercised less, compounding the problem.

Right around high school, I had moved in with my stepmom Tricia, who is writing the chapter you are reading. Tricia took over and sat me down to try and figure out how to curb my appetite. She knew I needed help and signed me up for a camp called Wellspring. The camp fosters health and well-being through a variety of techniques and not just dieting. Wellspring has a threefold approach. The first is learning to enjoy physical activity. The second is to eat healthy foods, foods that love you back. The third is more or less psychological, therapy to figure out what behaviors are triggering the weight gain.

At first, I was definitely like, "No, not a chance," but I warmed up to it. My dad, little brother, and I took a cross-country road trip to California to Wellspring. On the way, I was getting nervous about what was to come. The facility was set up with tents, and I shared a tent with another kid. Initially, I was shell shocked, thinking myself too fat to even try. It took a couple of days, and soon I was all-in having a great time. Ultimately, it was a great summer, a great first-time-away-from-home experience, which can easily be traumatic.

The camp helped me to get out of my comfort zone, which was a place where food was my solace. I began to feel more comfortable with my body and wanted to be healthier. I was really participating in a lifestyle change, not just changing eating habits. When I returned home after two months, I really knew I could succeed, although it's easier said than done. I went home with a positive attitude, determined to avoid bad eating habits and develop a healthy relationship with food, which was not easy.

I had a great freshman year in high school. But, soon I plateaued and the weight came back. For the next four years, I was up and down. I would become overwhelmed and turn back to my old eating habits. But, returning to Wellspring in the summer always got me back on track. I felt guilty about having to go back to camp and wound up attending four times. In my sophomore year the weight really came back on. Tricia and my dad were so supportive that I somehow had come to think that my success hinged on their praise and support, which was always abundant. At a certain point, though, I decided that my weight was no longer about my parents and that it was about me. I adjusted my outlook and took on my weight issues as my own personal mission.

Prior to returning to camp the third time, I had embraced once again the attitude that I could just eat anything I wanted. Arriving at camp I weighed 293 pounds. It was getting worse. At my second camp, I had weighed 260 pounds. Then, during my junior year of high school, I kept the weight off. I was determined that my senior year would be my finest year. I wanted to nip my weight in the bud, to be free of my weight problem in college. I wanted to be attractive for girls, to look good. One activity that really helped was running. I fell in love with running and carried that love into college, by which time I had dropped down to 185 pounds. I still had self-esteem issues and for some reason still saw myself as fat. I was successful but was not confident in my success.

So, off to college I went. I met my very first girlfriend and steadily gained confidence in myself while sticking to healthy food habits and continuing to run. But I slipped in my senior year. I started to party, began eating what I wanted, and to top it off broke my foot. I just let go of weight management as my focus. Of course, I gained weight. As you can tell, the journey was fraught with ups and downs, but that's typical. One just isn't simply cured. It's a lifelong effort to battle excess weight.

After college, I sat down and remembered the lessons from camp. I was in control of my fate. I had the tools necessary to be successful and soon got back into healthier habits. I really knocked down the pounds, feeling empowered once again. I decided that I wanted to help others with their weight and self-esteem and see what it was like from other side. In 2015, I went back to Wellspring as a camp counselor in Texas. I had the best time of my life. I could see exactly where the kids were coming from. I had been there. My own negative experiences and self-esteem issues went from negative to a positive. It was absolutely awesome to help those kids head in the right direction. Some kids were more motivated than others. The parents had made some of them attend. But, I had the mentality to help them lose the weight, develop healthy eating habits, enjoy physical activity, and recognize the behaviors that trigger overeating.

Recently, I returned to the camp, taking on a bigger role. The camp had picked up on mindfulness as a new weight-loss technique. One becomes mindful not only of what one eats, but through meditation one becomes aware of life events and behaviors that enforce bad habits. I was really stoked to see this new technique, not only for the kids but also for myself. I have been practicing mindfulness, and I can truly say that I am in better control of food and of those deep issues such as my parents' divorce. I want to help people, and I love working with kids. Helping others gives a tremendous reward. It reinforces your own motivation.

I'm still working through my issues, which are deeply rooted, such as always comparing myself to others, which leads to low self-esteem. Through continued practice of mindfulness, I am gaining more insight into my well-being. I was a psychology major in college and learned that we are creatures of habit. Since then, I've started to look more closely at the psychological aspects of my weight gain. For example, I notice I have some self-loathing, which society tends to encourage. I think everyone is subject to the cruel lens of society, which sees excess weight as a kind of personal fault. I still have self-image issues but am more okay with myself and can work on changing those negative thoughts.

So, as Tricia would second, I've had to take a hard look at my relationship with food. It's those little habits that make me struggle with my weight. Where did they come from? Why? Although I am prone to still fixate on the scales, the physical aspect of my weight gain is under control. I love life, and I'm coming to a better place every day.

One important aspect of losing weight is the idea of a calorie deficit. You should burn more calories than you take in. I really embraced physical activity after my fourth year of camp and physical activity became a way of life. To have a grasp of creating a calorie deficit, you have to know how many calories you are taking in and how many calories that you are burning. This involves recording calories and energy expenditure. It's hard at first to keep up with the information, but I soon found that I was addicted to burning calories and keeping track of my nutrition.

Coming back to mindfulness, I've developed a kind of intuitive eating, a mindful eating. I listen to my body but reject the notion of dieting. We should enjoy food and not feel guilty, especially when we are eating nutritious foods. I started to like eating vegetables and now enjoy eating nutritionally. Of course, I still enjoy eating cheeseburgers, but there is a balance. You shouldn't torture yourself over eating a cookie, but you should be mindful of how that cookie fits into your overall eating. I'm shifting now in my outlook on exercise as well. Instead of going to the gym to burn calories, I go to focus on how it makes me feel, to feel fit. Through mindfulness, my relationship with exercise is definitely healthier. I love to work out. It's a matter of seeking balance.

So, I'm now trusting in how good nutritional food can taste

and trusting in my mind and body to take care of me. I can't let my weight be the leading emotional factor in my life. Sure, I'm a lifetime weight manager and I still learn something new every day, but I'm in control of my weight. And I have to come back to Tricia. I think my journey for a better life would have ended quickly had it not been for her. She was my rock, especially in high school, when I needed her the most. Having that support, whether from a relative or friend, is really vital.

I DARE YOU—THE BOOK OF WISDOM

Whenever I come across an unexpected item offering a bit of wisdom that's relevant today or that I can apply in my own life, it makes me smile. In this case, it was a small book with an embossed checkerboard pattern and a silhouetted head. It was simply titled, *I Dare You!* The book had been written by William H. Danforth, the founder of Ralston Purina Company, and I happened to be perusing the seventeenth edition, dated May 1958.

With a little research, I learned that the first edition of this renowned self-help book was first published in 1931. People have been using it for the better part of a century. Born in 1870, Danforth founded Ralston Purina in 1894. The company's checkerboard logo that we know today actually relates to the principles of this book—his personal philosophy, the "Four Square" life. He believed that each person has not one, but four lives to live: physical, mental, social, and spiritual. The ingredients for life are a body, a brain, a heart, and a soul, Danforth would say. All four must grow in balance with each other.

A very busy executive, Danforth avoided letting business crowd out a happy balance of living. He made no secret of the fact that he took his health seriously and would proudly relate that he had never lost a day at the office on account of illness.

Walking a mile each day made him feel better, and his rule was to get eight hours of sleep a night with the windows open. He ate moderately and controlled his weight.

In the first few pages of the book, he states that health is the foundation for individual success and a nation's progress. I couldn't agree more. In fact, I'm completely focused on wellness and nutrition and realize how important it is to incorporate this into everyday life to remain productive. As a progressive thinker, Danforth was already on this path in 1931.

Written for both the individual's personal and professional life, here are a few excerpts of Danforth's self-help wisdom:

Daring people can't afford not to think. The big prizes are for those who dare to think hard, to think often, to think creatively. Today, ideas get an audience immediately.

When you make a new contact, it doesn't take long to write a note showing that you appreciated it. It isn't any gift you send, it's the thought that goes with it that endears you to others.

Adventurous spirits will meet obstacles, but dare to map out a program of life with a sense of direction, but with no sense of obstacles.

So how did I acquire this book? My father. He had been a fan of the wisdom of Danforth and had given his copy to me. As my dad became more ill, I would discuss the passages and purpose with him and how relative it was in my world. There were many passages of importance, but there are two key things that I have learned to embrace. First, understand who you are talking to and what's important to them. Put yourself in the other person's shoes. Second, don't be afraid to step forward. Without being arrogant, have the attitude that you are at least as good as the other person, and when you have a good thought, present it.

Over the years, Danforth saw many bright people trail behind because they were not bold in presenting their ideas at the right time. These people defeated themselves—they didn't dare.

Turn toward your strengths, not your weaknesses. Wake up in the morning thinking of ways to do things, rather than reasons why they can't be done.

The book's wisdom has taught me a lot. And it's shown me that I'm well on my way to leading a "Four Square" life, one that I wish for you.

Next, we have Carol's story.

CAROL'S STORY

Let me tell you about Carol, a colleague of mine who knows the unconditional acceptance that a dog can bring. Carol is a canine blogger and is openly gay. She has been with Darlene for twenty-five years, legally and happily married since 2015. When she was younger, she was always afraid of what others would think and lost some friends over her sexual orientation but found real friendship and comfort from her Cocker Spaniel puppy, Brandy. Brandy was the runt of the litter, cowering in the corner. Carol says that Brandy picked her, which is often the case when adopting a dog.

Still "in the closet" at the time, Carol says that Brandy taught her how to slow down and savor life. When Brandy died after fifteen years, Carol experienced overwhelming grief and depression. The pain was so intense that she vowed never again to open her heart to such trauma as losing a best friend and entered grief counseling. But, that reluctance only lasted thirty days.

Dexter, another Cocker Spaniel, found her, and the outlet she needed to love and care for another being was discovered again. She then established a group called WiggleButt Warriors and raised over $50,000 to help homeless dogs. It was on her blog that Carol opened up to the world. Dogs she says, do not care about your color, gender, or sexual orientation, and that's so true. Dexter was the best man at her wedding. He accepted her for who she really was. Carol even has a tattoo that says, "My Heart Beats Dog." With her blog, she continues to advocate for homeless dogs and offers practical advice on how best to raise and live with your best friend. With dogs, the world is a better place. Dogs bring out the best in us humans, and we deserve that affirmation. It's so important to find that love and then to pass it on, to pay it forward, as Beckie does in this next story.

BECKIE'S STORY

Beckie is a good friend and works with me helping clients achieve better lives with their dogs. She is a veterinary technician by trade and often sees dogs that are overweight with overweight owners. Beckie is a dog lover, of course, and has five dogs, all rescues, who love her unconditionally. Her oldest is a German Shepherd named Bocephus who had heartworm disease when she adopted him. She also rescued two chi-weenies from a shopping cart at Walmart.

Beckie routinely sees obese dogs suffering from diabetes, degenerative joints, and asthma. Beckie notes that owners will often give cute names to fat dogs. One of her most successful patients was a mutt named Skinny Vinny who weighed forty-five pounds when he should have weighed only seventeen pounds. Beckie put him on a weight-loss program, and now Skinny Vinny is healthy and happy.

Beckie knows that we often love our dogs through food. I've often said that you have to walk a mile in the shoes of others to understand why others act and feel the way they do. Beckie says that owners often don't realize the harm they are doing to their pets by overfeeding and need someone to offer practical dietary advice. Many dog owners may suffer from emotional or mental disorders or simply feel that society has somehow rejected them. A dog enters their life and loves them for just being themselves. It's only natural to love that dog back, sometimes in the form of too much food and too many treats.

Through nutritional counseling and physical activity, Beckie is transforming lives. When we love a dog with food to the point that it can't even clean itself, we often need that extra help that someone like Beckie can provide. And Beckie would be the first to admit that she too has suffered from weight problems, as have I, and she understands where owners are coming from. She knows too well the tendency to just laugh off obesity as a "few holiday pounds."

Beckie is eternally optimistic and helps clients treat their dogs with the respect they deserve. Whether it's working with children with autism or veterans suffering from PTSD, Beckie is able to bridge the gaps left by disease and hurt to bring out the best in others. Dogs only see the good in people, Beckie says. And, she's right.

Next is Andrea's story.

ANDREA'S STORY

Andrea credits her dogs Bandit, Lilly, and Cookie with inspiring her to become a canine trainer. She has been teaching since 2002 and has had animals all of her life. Her own dogs suffered a variety of health problems, including hip problems, injured tendons, and even cancer. Through those experiences, she has built a life of caring for dogs and their owners.

At first, she struggled, not really knowing how to piece it all together. How do you address behavioral issues, teach obedience, and cure physical ailments? With her own dogs, her training has paid off in good ways. Like many of us, her dogs behaved badly on walks and fought with each other inside the house. She has learned that fitness reinforces obedience and leads to healthier relationships among dogs and their owners. She has learned that fit dogs are happier and more well-adjusted, and that applies to people too.

In working with her clients, she has learned that everyone, every dog, is different and that she has to remain versatile and open to what each needs. Owners often start with their own needs in mind, but soon realize that it's best to put the dog's interest first. Working out with your dog encourages selflessness and a better outlook on life as a whole. While owners are stretching and engaging their dogs in physical activity and games, the bond between them is strengthened.

When asked what advice she gives owners, the answers may be surprising. She advises that we find out what motivates our best friends, our dogs, and then reinforce behaviors attached to those motivations. Often what motivates best is simple praise, a few kind words and a friendly back scratch. As a trainer, she realizes that owners must manage their dog's fitness and take an active role in their well-being, which is priceless when the rewards follow.

A BETTER YOU, A BETTER DOG, A BETTER LIFE

I hope that these stories inspire you and motivate you to make some positive changes in your life and your dog's life. I know that you can do it. The journey can at times be a struggle but remember that we are with you the entire way. It takes courage and knowledge to make healthy choices, and you are on the right path to making that happen. Now that you have the motivational foundation for your first thirty days to happiness with your best friend, your dog, Dr. Ernie Ward will guide you along a path to better nutrition, which will make you and your dog feel better and will result in real health benefits, both mental and physical.

WEEK TWO: NUTRITION, WEIGHT, AND OPTIMAL HEALTH

—Dr. Ernie Ward—

My primary goal is to enhance the lives and well-being of pets and people. That ambitious goal is why I became a veterinarian and why I've dedicated much of my career to the fight against pet and human obesity. For me, striving for that optimal health state means making life more fulfilling and meaningful through finding motivation, wholesome nutrition, appropriate physical activity, and building community for emotional support. Together we can discover and identify the disease risks of obesity and formulate a plan to address them, ultimately expanding you and your dog's life to its fullest extent. You deserve it and your dog does as well.

By raising awareness of health issues related to nutrition and physical activity, we can change our behavior for the better. I want to improve your quality of life versus chasing a number on a scale. Ultimately, it's a joy to improve your diet and physical fitness, to move, to interact with your dog and others and enjoy life to its fullest. Can we take your dog and help him bound up the steps as he did when younger? Can we make you feel better and more energetic by eating healthy foods? The answer is a resounding Yes! We want to be happy, and we want our dogs to be happy as well. So, let me introduce you to Chester, a hefty bulldog that changed the way I see and treat canine obesity to improve a pet's quality of life.

CHESTER'S STORY

I vividly remember hearing Chester, a colossal bulldog, before I saw him. This was early in my career in 1997. I had been out of vet school for five years and had become more confident. I was optimistic and knew that the status quo wasn't good enough. I was becoming frustrated with the mindset in veterinary medicine of largely ignoring the nutrition and lifestyle of my patients.

That morning, Chester the bulldog was snorting and snuffling as he shuffled along, expending a tremendous effort to put one leg in front of the other. Immediately I thought, *This dog is in distress.* Chester took his time waddling into my exam room. That moment became a pivotal point in my veterinary career. I realized, "This isn't normal." Chester's owners didn't think anything was unusual about their blundering bulldog. My staff saw Chester as any other bulldog that ate too much and played too little. After all, weren't bulldogs supposed to snort, shuffle, and sashay? Didn't all bulldogs gain weight, have an assortment of ailments, and ultimately live shorter lives? That was when I said, "Not necessarily. We can do better." And so began my journey with Chester.

Chester was seeing me that day for his annual wellness visit and labs. The owners were in a playful mood, absent any worries about Chester's health. Meanwhile, I was having a professional existential crisis. What was I really doing? Was I enhancing life, preventing disease, or simply adhering to medical dogma that treated every patient as a "dog" instead of a "unique individual?" Health is more than the absence of illness. My responsibility wasn't simply to diagnose disease but to prevent it, to improve Chester's well-being. My career was about to get very interesting and a whole lot more complicated.

Reviewing Chester's examination findings, I began probing beyond the standard discussion of vaccines, heartworm prevention, and diet. I asked questions such as "Can he get up the stairs? Can he get into the car? How is his sleeping?" I soon discovered his owners had gone to incredible lengths to accommodate Chester. They used a board to help him step up into the car that partially blocked one of the rear passenger seats, making for some uncomfortable trips. They had placed carpet runners over their beautiful bamboo floor to help him walk easier. Chester's dad had even injured his back, hoisting Chester up the back steps on a cold February morning when the bulldog's joints were overburdened and achy. It may have been the overconfidence of youth, but I basically said to the owners, "You know, we can do better for Chester. With your help, I believe we can help Chester feel like a puppy again."

They seemed to realize Chester wasn't living his best life and agreed to change Chester's diet. Apparently, Chester (like many dogs) loved sausages and pizza and never met a treat he didn't devour. In addition to switching to a therapeutic weight-loss dog food, measuring food and calculating calories, we agreed that Chester's treats would consist of carrots and crunchy vegetables. It's easy to tell your veterinarian you'll make these changes, but could they actually do it with the help of my team?

Amazingly, Chester's owners kept their promise to return for weight checks, count calories, and stuck with the new feeding habits. It was a year-long journey for Chester to lose the weight that was preventing him from fully enjoying his life. In that year, Chester lost twelve pounds, from a staggering sixty-four pounds down to a more manageable fifty-two pounds. That was our goal, to lose those twelve pounds. Those twelve pounds not only improved Chester's quality of life, but also the life of his pet parents and inspired me to change my outlook on medicine and health.

Chester's success validated that I could help other dogs affected by obesity. Sure, Chester was like any other dog that needed vaccines and routine veterinary care, but from that day, I knew I needed to actively address each patient's quality of life. Chester's weight was no longer simply a number on a scale; it was an indicator of well-being. After a year, Chester became a dog that could get into the car without assistance or sound like a vacuum cleaner—like many flat-nosed dogs—enjoy walks in the park, and play with other dogs. Those improvements amounted to a small miracle. The owners were able to eventually remove the ramp Chester needed to amble up the back-porch steps (the same steps that caused Chester's dad to hurt his back). Chester was living more independently, and his owners believed he was happier. There was no magic diet, no secret exercise, just systematic, slow changes that evolved into a lifestyle.

Through Chester, I saw how beating obesity can create a very real improvement in quality of life, what I came to call life enhancement. After weight loss, Chester's owners felt he was a different dog. Watching Chester improve gave them confidence, and they realized that short-nosed breeds don't have to live with constant discomfort and fatigue. I observed how successful weight loss enhanced the human-animal bond. Chester was my first serious weight-loss success case, giving me confidence to become more involved with all of my cases of obesity and overweight.

As veterinarians and pet parents, we have to reset our understanding of "normal." It's not normal to be miserable and huffing and puffing for oxygen. It's not normal for a dog to be unable to walk around the block due to excess weight. It's not normal for pets to have their lives cut short by the consequences of excess fat tissues. It's not normal to suffer and experience poor quality of life due to poor nutrition and obesity. The simple realization of "This isn't normal. He's not just big-boned. I will not accept this quality of life for my pet patients" changed how I practiced veterinary medicine. Over time, we tend to lower our expectations and standards of "normal" and ultimately contribute to our dogs' suffering. It is vitally important that we look at our pets and ask, "Am I really doing the best for my best friend?"

LAYING THE GROUNDWORK

In Week One, Tricia has done a fantastic job of motivating you toward a *Better You, Better Dog, Better Life,* which is week one of your journey. Let me build on that for a moment before we dive into nutrition. I've said that I like to think in terms of life enhancement, a better quality of life for you and your dog. We should always be striving for an optimal health state. Good health isn't just the absence of illness. When you feel great and your dog feels great, life is more fulfilling and meaningful. What I hope to do is raise your awareness to the reality of optimal health through proper nutrition and regular physical activity. This comes at a relatively small price: eating healthy foods in the right proportions and daily movements such as walking and play. And the benefits are immeasurable: you and your dog will feel better, have fewer medical conditions, and enjoy a higher quality of life.

Of course, it's important to take this in context. You or your dog may have pre-existing health problems or disease risks that require modifications of the methods of nutrition and fitness we describe for you. For example, if you or your dog suffers from high blood pressure, it's going to be important that you monitor your sodium intake. If your dog is obese, she'll need to take shorter, slower walks at first. But, let's work on creating a general mindset that supports your journey to happiness with your beloved canine. The details are critical, but it's the purpose that will guide you. Having said that, don't imagine yourself chasing a number on the scales or a pant's size. That's not what we're here to do. We're here to enjoy life with our pets. Your goal should be to see your dog trot with a lively step versus panting and laboring. Embrace a purpose to see you through the challenges you and your dog will encounter.

I also have obese clients who come to me to help their dog with obesity. I strive to be a judgement-free veterinarian. I'm not there to focus on the pet parent's medical condition but am always surprised at how their dog's healthy habits often influence their own. As a veterinarian, my primary obligation is to help my pet patients, but often healthy habits rub off on the owners as well. It's essential that pet parents don't feel judged or shamed in any way by a veterinary professional. That's often easier said than done, but please understand that your veterinarian is there to help your pet, not make you feel embarrassed. I'm sure that veterinarians and physicians occasionally cross that line and behave badly, but before you become upset with your own doctor or veterinary healthcare team, be certain they intend no harm.

Over the years, I've had a couple of clients respond negatively after I diagnosed their pet with obesity. "What are you saying? Are you blaming me for this? Are you accusing me of not being a good pet owner? Are you saying this because I'm obese?" No, I'm telling you this because I want to help. I want your pet, and you, to live a long, disease-free life. It's not a judgment about you or your health; it's simply a fact, and we have to constructively deal with it.

In many cases, a pet owner absorbs the diet and exercise information and begins applying it to their own health. When I recommend an activity program, typically the owner gets more active as well. By paying attention to nutrition for their dog, many pet parents begin altering their own diet. We can address many pet nutritional myths and misunderstandings, many of which are similar in human nutrition. Many of the nutritional strategies we use in dogs, especially high-protein, low-carbohydrate weight-loss programs, also work for people. The special connection we have with our pets offers veterinarians the opportunity to positively influence human health while serving their pet patients. I'd like to share an example of that idea in practice through two of my tiny friends, Henrietta and Betsy.

HENRIETTA'S AND BETSY'S STORY

Henrietta and Betsy were two female Chihuahuas. The best way to describe the two pooches is that they were owned by an overweight widow, and they perfectly mirrored the shape of their owner. The widow, I'll call her Ann, had moved down to North Carolina from New York to be near the beach and had adopted Henrietta and Betsy to help fill the gap of her lost spouse. She was a lovely lady, and I had to ask myself, "Do I really want go there? Do I confront this cute, little, older lady, struggling with her own weight about her dogs' obesity?" I could just imagine her sitting on a couch with a box of sweets, dispensing one for her and one for each of the dogs.

Ann walked into my life about five years after Chester's case, and I was up to the challenge. In this case, with a new client experiencing her own set of stressful issues (recently widowed, moved, and probably dealing with her own set of emotional challenges), I hesitated calling attention to the dogs' obesity. But it was my professional obligation to speak up for the pets, while being compassionate and respectful to Ann. I always imagine my pet patients speaking: "Dr. Ernie, I need help with my weight. I feel terrible. Can you do something?"

Because of their ample size, only one dog could sit in Ann's lap at a time. They took turns panting on the floor and panting in her lap. They wanted to be carried nearly everywhere, because they would nearly collapse if pushed to walk more than a few yards. Their weight was in the teens, more than double their ideal body weight, which is considered morbid obesity. I started by saying, "I can tell how much you care about your dogs. Because you love them so much, we need to talk about their weight." I saw Ann bristle. She replied, "What do you mean, obesity?"

As a veterinarian dedicated to combatting obesity, I didn't just see the two Chihuahuas as "fat" or "obese," but battling a disease, suffering with pain, and doomed to a shorter, poorer quality of life. I was very concerned. Chihuahuas, as a breed, have a higher incidence of back issues, heart disease, high blood pressure, and cancer. Henrietta and Betsy were young at the time, but there was no way they would survive ten or fifteen years in this condition. There was simply no way around these facts, and I had to help Ann realize that. As a veterinarian, it can be difficult to gauge how a client accepts my diagnosis or my recommendations. I can provide advice and guidance, but the owner must act on it. So, we explored together what would be best for her pups, starting with nutrition and physical activity. At the end of our time, she said, "Thank you," and that was that. I had made my case and now waited for the jury to return a verdict.

My staff told me, "You'll never budge this one. She's battling obesity, her husband has recently passed, and she has no emotional support network nearby." On cue (and quite a shock for my team), exactly one week later, Ann returned with Henrietta and Betsy for thyroid testing, which I had recommended before we embarked on dietary changes. That was step one. It was a big one. She was concerned. She had accepted my advice. She recognized that her dogs *were* her support network, and she needed to protect and preserve them. The next day, I called her back with the great news that the dogs' blood tests were normal. That meant we had a great opportunity to make a serious change through diet, physical activity, and lifestyle improvements. We diagnosed obesity relatively early. Obesity is a disease, and we could tackle this together. Now my work really began.

When I said, "Let's talk more about diet," the most amazing thing happened. She interrupted, "Stop there, Dr. Ernie. You just tell me exactly what I need to do to make them live as long as possible." What she was saying is "These dogs are all I've got. I've lost so much, and I can't lose these precious things. Let's do this." She turned out to be a model pet owner, doing everything I recommended. By following a few simple rules, which turned out to be limited physical activity (15-minute walks each day to start) and better nutrition (a high-protein, low-carb therapeutic diet and veggie treats), Henrietta and Betsy began to slim down and perk up.

Two years later, the dogs had lost significant weight and looked and acted so differently—pain free, energetic, independent, healthy, and happy. And they both could sit on Ann's lap at the same time!

Sadly, Ann did not take the advice for herself. It was Ann who developed diabetes and high blood pressure. There was a point when she could not walk her dogs, and she had to hire neighborhood kids to help. Eventually, Ann had to undergo several painful amputation surgeries and moved into an assisted living facility near her daughter.

Ann taught me another important lesson. When I'm dealing with pet obesity, there are people who will go to extraordinary lengths for their pet, but not for themselves. Or, it works the other way. I've had marathon moms in prime health who bring in their 105-pound lab but don't walk their dog. I've had nutritionists who insist on feeding poor quality foods and ignoring their pet's obesity. You can imagine an entire spectrum of possibilities, some easier to deal with than others. Tricia, David, and I want the best quality of life for you and your pet. I don't promise a magic pill, secret sauce, or simple solution to cure obesity. Obesity is a complex medical disorder that requires multiple often simultaneous approaches to defeat. But the battle is worth it, at least for Chester, Henrietta, and Betsy, and countless other dogs who've endured the journey and emerged victorious.

CANINE NUTRITION

I love dogs, and I love canine nutrition. As a veterinarian, I witness the impact obesity has on our best friends. As the founder of the Association for Pet Obesity Prevention (APOP), I am dedicated to fighting a rising trend in dog obesity. According to APOP research, at least 56 percent of dogs in the United States are overweight or obese. Think about it, one out of two dogs are at risk of preventable diseases such as diabetes, arthritis, high blood pressure, kidney disease, and cancer. If your dog is suffering from the chronic effects of excess fat tissues, I'm here to help you fight this disease and restore your beloved pet's health and vitality. We share a unique and special bond with our dogs, and we owe them a comfortable and healthy life. How do we get motivated to change? How do we bring your pet back to a healthy weight?

    I think that in motivating for change there is a classic approach that most veterinarians and physicians use—fear. Although well intentioned, trying to scare pet owners into action is probably not the best approach, especially for lasting change and long-term health. Sure, a dog with obesity is at great risk for diseases such as joint disorders or cancer, but what I've found in my career is that fear only works to a limited degree with a select group. Goading a pet owner with fear can be a real turnoff. Fear-based approaches primarily instill guilt, and pet owners may feel like I am holding a hammer over their head (or even hitting them in the head). There is no need to be ashamed or guilty about obesity. You are not intentionally harming your dog, so much as perhaps loving them too much by overfeeding or giving too many treats. Overfeeding generally comes from a place of love, so how can feeding be bad?

What I have found useful is to state the facts and be emotionally supportive and empathetic. We have to reframe pet obesity treatment into a manageable approach, aiming toward wellness, while recognizing the serious consequences of obesity as a disease. When I see a dog with obesity, I see illness, but I also see a cure. I see simple, practical measures that bring relief and enhance life. I think, "How does this animal feel? Does she feel tired? Does she have less energy? Does she have the motivation to play?" I really try and dig into the emotional and psychological realm of the dog. I am the interpreter for this animal. It's my job to reach a deeper understanding of my pet patients, working closely with the owner. It's a key step for the owner to see obesity through the eyes and heart of their pet.

So, first, how does a dog with obesity feel? How do you think he feels? It becomes a matter of empathizing with the animal, working toward positive change. Fear and guilt only make pet parents feel bad, encourages them to make excuses, blame others, and ultimately does little to effect change. I want to pursue hope, encourage love, and offer solutions. When you understand that obesity is affecting your pet's quality of life, how he feels, you become motivated to bring more happiness into his life. If we can say, "My dog feels terrible, his mind is slow, he lacks motivation to play with his toys, and his joints are achy," this is an important first step. You are becoming truly empathetic, taking charge and feeling empowered to bring about change.

Second, it's not enough for me to dispense advice. As parents do with human children, you are making the daily decisions that affect your pet's health. Sure, I'm here to guide you, to give you real tips that work, but I'm also here to support both you and your dog emotionally. Without support, good intentions often end up nowhere. That's why the final chapter of this book, Week Four—Building Community, is so important. I can help you begin you this journey, but for long-term, sustainable results, surrounding yourself with people who share the passion for pet health is needed. It can be as simple as having a friend walk dogs with you. It's okay to need help, and my job is to give you permission to ask for that help. I want success for you and your pet. What matters most is that you begin this journey and that you have the confidence to carry it forward, regardless of obstacles and challenges. My job is to embrace the emotional connection you have with your pet, to help you develop the nutritional techniques for weight loss, and to encourage a community of support in order to sustain optimal health. Let me tell you about Lucky.

LUCKY'S STORY

Dachshunds make great companions. They're intelligent, friendly, protective, and are exceptional slow walkers. Looking for a stroll-buddy? Sausage dogs may be your best choice. But the Dachshund's long body can create problems with their back, especially if they are overweight or obese. Lucky was one such unlucky dog.

I knew Lucky's owner, Sheila, from the gym. She was CrossFit muscled and had a tattoo of an eagle perched on her shoulder. I was under the impression she could lift more than

I could, probably much more. In one short veterinary visit, I learned Sheila was born in New Jersey, went to college in Illinois, had three brothers, and was recently divorced. She had brought Lucky with her from the marriage, rescuing her from a "textbook train wreck of a husband." Lucky was a typical bronze, floppy-eared Doxie, unafraid and outgoing, and prone to yipping at strangers, including my staff. Sheila took excellent care of Lucky, except when it came to her diet. I estimated Lucky's ideal weigh to be sixteen pounds, but she weighed twenty-eight, which I considered serious obesity.

It turned out that Sheila was loving her pet to death through food. Lucky was a fast-food junkie, even though Shelia ate relatively healthy. She would take Lucky for rides in her SUV and make pit stops at fast-food joints, buying her cheeseburgers, which she would wolf down in the car. At home, Lucky would gobble her food, and Sheila would just fill the bowl until Lucky could eat no more. It was obvious to me that Sheila was devastated by her divorce, having been set adrift into uncertainty about her life, and that poor Lucky was the receptacle for her grief. Lucky's back sagged, and she was in obvious pain when she walked into my clinic.

After easing Sheila into the pet obesity conversation, I began the delicate discussion about the best plan to relieve Lucky's painful spinal condition. Without batting an eye, she frowned and confessed the back pain was caused by Lucky's weight gain, and she was to blame. She admitted to overfeeding Lucky and agreed it had to stop. Fortunately, I didn't have to be the bearer of bad news because Sheila knew what had to be done. She just needed a little confrontation to create change. We then began reviewing nutritional strategies to ensure Lucky could have the best chance at many years of pain-free life.

We worked out a plan of measuring Lucky's food, a hundred or so milligrams twice a day of a high-protein therapeutic diet and no more fast food treats. With such a voracious appetite, I was confident Lucky would easily enjoy healthy, low-calorie snacks and encouraged Sheila to try a variety of crunchy vegetables to see what Lucky liked best (baby carrots and zucchini slices). Because Lucky was such a central part of her life, we also discussed the possibility of home cooking meals for Lucky, focusing on lean meat and vegetables, similar to what she prepared for herself. It's certainly not necessary that you cook for your dog in order to help them lose weight, but it is an option if you have the time and inclination. In my book, *Chow Hounds*, I provide a list of recipes and "people foods" that interested owners can incorporate into their dog's diet. In the back of this book, I've provided a few of my favorite recipes. Planning meals a week in advance and cooking bulk meals for freezing can often result in healthier diets and may actually reduce your pet food costs.

Sheila liked the idea of cooking for Lucky. She already cooked for herself but was honest and said that she doubted that she could home-cook all of Lucky's meals, which is fine. Ultimately, we agreed on my Hybrid Menu (more on that later) in which Sheila would cook for Lucky when she could and then properly ration a therapeutic, high-protein, low-carb weight-loss food the rest of the time.

I saw Lucky three months later, and she had already lost five pounds, which, considering her overall weight, was quite significant. Our plan was working! I was thrilled, and Sheila was overjoyed. Lucky's back pain had eased, and she was able to go on short walks without resorting to lying down on the sidewalk halfway around the block due to discomfort. It's been awhile since I've seen Lucky, and I'm hopeful that she has lost even more weight.

I ask you to do what Sheila did: Ask yourself what you can do for your best friend to make her happier and healthier. You might be surprised when some of that advice rubs off on you.

THE FIRST SEVEN DAYS OF BETTER NUTRITION

Let's take a look at your first seven days of optimizing both your and your pet's nutrition. Let me emphasize that this is not a weight-loss program. This is a quality of life program. In Week One, you've already had the benefit of Tricia's motivation, and now for Week Two it's time to put that motivation into real action.

First, let's examine some quality of life issues your dog may be confronting. Does your dog experience difficulty climbing stairs or getting in and out of a car? Do you have to help your dog jump on the bed or couch? Is your pet easily winded by walking briskly for a few minutes? These may be signs that excess weight and poor nutrition are slowing your pet down and adversely affecting quality of life.

I want to emphasize that we are working toward goals that are achievable. We begin by setting realistic goals based on activity and lifestyle. Let's say that within six months, our goal is that your dog can jump onto the bed or couch by herself. That's something you can see and measure as a success. With each small improvement, we're moving toward our larger goal of reducing disease risk and extending longevity. While you are enjoying the small victories, your dog is shedding excess body fat. You are ridding yourself and your dog of the real underlying danger: excess fat and the chronic inflammation it produces. You are decreasing the risk of a wide variety of health and performance issues and improving quality of life. Research concludes that dogs losing as little as 6 percent of body mass experience an improvement in quality of life and vitality [9]. That's a goal worthy of a little effort.

It's okay, often desirable, to start a weight-loss program

slowly. Using physical activity as an example, start by walking your dog around the block. This may seem simple, but it's necessary to build on small successes. Next, walk around the block twice, then three times, working your way up to a continuous, brisk walk for thirty minutes. In Week Three—Physical Activity and Optimal Health, David will put you on the right track to optimize your and your dog's physical activity needs. So, for now, let's get back to nutrition.

We are primarily interested here in a seven-day plan to begin a lifelong change in eating and feeding habits. Eventually, the rate of weight loss and restoration of mobility and strength are going to slow down. This first week is needed to get you into the mindset of healthy eating and daily habits that you follow in the months and years ahead. During this first week, we are going to learn to calculate calories. Every food has a caloric value and excess calories are stored in the body as fat, which is what we want to avoid.

Don't be misled into thinking this requires a lot of extra effort. It's really very simple. Using a kitchen scale or cup measure, feed your dog the portion needed as calculated by your veterinarian or recommended on the dog food bag. The majority of dogs are fed dry kibble, and they're fed too much. Your dog's food bowl should not be a bottomless buffet. Make sure one person in your home is responsible for feeding your dog. Mindfully measure and dispense each meal. I call this "food-bowl awareness" and this mindset is critical to successful pet weight loss. A dog that has access to nearly unlimited food (or treats) will most likely eat what it is given, so control is up to you. I see far too many pet owners who plead, "But my dog pesters me for food!" Your pet is relying on you to take the best care of him or her, not yield to their every unhealthy desire. Every act of feeding your dog, and yourself, should involve thoughtful, conscious, mindful decisions and actions.

Better you, Better Dog, Better life

What about treats? Treats are typically nothing more than excess, nutritionally-vacant calories and need to be carefully considered. I get it; you feel your dog loves you when you give him a treat, but it's primarily the act of giving (and receiving) that makes him happy. To most humans, the act of treating is about the food; to most dogs, it's about the attention.

When it comes to treats, we need to discuss the role of real, nutritious whole foods instead of highly-processed junk food treats. I recommend and feed my own dogs baby carrots, sliced cucumbers and zucchini, broccoli, and green beans. These foods are packed with powerful phytonutrients and contain few calories. I know it's tempting to feed a little pizza crust whenever your beloved dog stares at your Italian pie but return the loving gaze and offer a healthy snack and a pat on the head. Don't feel guilty; feel good knowing you're making a little decision that can have big health benefits. Exchanging pizza crust for baby carrots can end up boosting your pet's quality of life.

It's important to remember your dog craves you more than food. Your attention, interaction, and praise mean more to your dog than any dog biscuit or pizza crust. Instead of reaching for a junk-food treat, praise your dog. Rub her ears and scratch her back. Go for a walk or throw a ball. I suggest you "praise and play" when you feed a healthy snack to reinforce that your love is associated with nourishment. Some dogs may hold out for cookies over carrots at first; be persistent. If carrots aren't your pooch's prize, try different vegetables such as a slice of cucumber or zucchini. Try offering vegetables raw or slightly cooked, cool or warm, soft or crunchy. Different dogs will like different treats, but always accompany food rewards with generous praise. It's the act of you giving that matters most to dogs, and dogs love our praise most of all.

By the end of the first week, I suggest you begin weighing your dog's meals for precise portions. I understand not everyone will break out the food scales, but I strongly encourage you to consider it. If you need to, give yourself a month of portioning your dog's food with a measuring cup and then take it to the next, more accurate level of weight. If you continue feeding dry food, you'll quickly learn what the ideal portions weigh. I've included an appendix (Appendix One) in the back of the book called "Typical Feeding Guide." This will help you earn "food-bowl awareness," which is an important daily habit. Weighing the food with a simple kitchen scale will closely control calories, leaving little room for inadvertent dispensing errors. The first couple of weeks it may seem like a burden, but it takes less time than to lace your shoes and reinforces the practice of mindful feeding.

During this first week, I also want you to do something else that adds to your emerging food-bowl awareness. I want you to begin a brief feeding diary. Every time you feed your dog or give a treat, record it. You may want to do the same thing for yourself. One page for the dog, and one page for you. If a written diary seems like too much trouble, make a habit of taking a picture of the food or treat with your cell phone, before you give it to the dog. This makes you consider the act of feeding that follows. Why does this work so well? It makes you acutely aware of what foods are going into your dog's body. You don't want to feel guilty every time you feed your dog, but you're beginning to develop an essential state of mindful feeding. Recording your pet's food intake also lets you know when you might be cheating by giving too many extra calories. Give it a try.

So, you're thinking, I have to measure food, record it, and exercise with my dog, all at once? One thing that I have learned over twenty-five years as a veterinarian is that good habits grow gradually. In Week Three, David is going to begin you on a path to physical fitness but let me emphasize that your first goal is to improve both your own and your pet's nutrition. We're taking this journey slowly. Take David's advice seriously, but in many cases exercise follows initial weight loss and lifestyle changes. Although daily physical activity is critical to optimal health and a natural partner of good nutrition, nutrition should come first for weight loss then followed by routine physical activity.

There is flexibility in any weight-loss program; stay focused on what you're able to do versus what you can't. With your increasing food-bowl awareness, your dog will begin to safely lose weight and adding exercise will increase additional weight loss and improve lean muscle mass and fitness. I have discovered the hard way, that if you throw everything at a pet owner at once, it's often overwhelming and leads to failure. During these first thirty days, we are easing you into the process. When there's too much to do, it can be hard to begin. Start simply. Each seemingly insignificant change builds on the next, and soon you've built a solid framework of good healthy habits. You'll find yourself not wanting to cut corners but finding ways to do more to enhance your and your pet's life. This is your opportunity to be the hero your pet deserves. Now, let's hear about Rosie.

ROSIE'S STORY

Rosie was an ageing retriever. Her owners were overworked parents in their late thirties, with three kids, two high-powered jobs, and no time for much else. Years ago, they decided their kids needed a dog, not pondering the considerable responsibilities of owning a pet. By the time I met her, Rosie had become what I call a "yard ornament." She looked great with the white picket fence and manicured lawn in the Christmas photos but in reality received little to no playtime, exercise, or interaction. To lessen their guilt over not spending time with Rosie, the family fed her tons of dog treats. Giving treats satisfies our need to please our pets. It's like saying, "Hey, I'm being nice to you," but with minimal effort. And Rosie wasn't complaining as long as her bowl was perpetually packed.

Rosie was an overlooked victim of the twenty-first-century rat race and soon developed obesity. Even the family cat was diagnosed with obesity. When I first saw Rosie, she was morbidly obese at ninety-five pounds when she should have weighed sixty-five to seventy pounds. Rosie was a shadow of her former gorgeous self, with a coarse, dry coat, a lighter shade of lusterless gold. I still thought she was beautiful, albeit dulled by the side effects of obesity. I could tell that Rosie came from a strong, robust line of golden retrievers, and I committed myself to restoring her health and vitality. When we met, her eyes sparkled in a hopeful manner. I believed Rosie was an intelligent being and sensed she'd been shuffled aside. I must admit I felt quite sorry for her. Her eyes seemed to say, "Why don't they take me outside to play? Isn't there more to life than my backyard, bed, and bowl?" I think she knew I wanted to help.

This first encounter with Rosie was for her annual checkup. I raised the notion that Rosie had obesity and the mom responded with a huff and rolled her eyes. She fired back with how busy her days were. "I get up at five a.m. to check my work e-mails and get my two kids ready for school. I work eight to ten hours a day and still have work to do over the weekend. My daughter takes two different styles of dance classes, and my son has soccer three days a week. My husband has…" Hers was a typical response of a successful family, but the bottom line is that she was making excuses for not having time for Rosie. Instead of judging or making unreasonable (and unachievable) requests, I focused on strategies to help Rosie that required little time and effort. I learned that the owner purchased the cheapest dog food, not because she couldn't afford better diets, but because Rosie could, and would, eat anything without issue. In addition to an arguably poor diet choice, she told me the kids often snuck Rosie what was left on their plates. Her husband also had little time, and Rosie was, naturally, last in line for their time and energy. The owner was doing the best she could and wasn't sure what else she might realistically do. Rosie was just a dog, after all.

I said, "Here's the deal. There are some very simple things we can do. I'm going to make this incredibly quick and easy for you and your family to follow these instructions. You can do it!" Despite my promise, the mom stuck to her story of being pressed for time. I knew this was going to be a tough case, so I scrambled for an easy victory to prove it could work. I focused on the issue of Rosie's endless treats and recommended that she substitute a baby carrot instead of a boxed treat, at least once a day. To my surprise, she agreed. I must admit I was a bit skeptical, fearing she was looking for an excuse to get out of my office.

Two months later, Rosie returned with an ear infection. Guess what? Rosie had lost three pounds with no substantive dietary change, just a hint of mindfulness of how many treats they were feeding her. I was ecstatic and enthusiastically congratulated her success. The owner shrugged and remarked that Rosie seemed to love the carrots, and they were cheaper than the processed treats she'd been giving, so she'd probably keep giving them. No fanfare or happiness, but I sensed she was proud of the change she had made with Rosie. She had taken action and changed a simple behavior. And three pounds lost is three pounds fewer health risks for Rosie.

That day I also realized Rosie's owner was very attentive and decide to probe a little further: How much food was she feeding Rosie each day? She wasn't exactly sure—maybe two to three cups twice a day? I had a simple request. I asked her to reduce Rosie's food by half a cup per meal, no effort or extra time needed. I knew they were grossly overfeeding Rosie and half a cup less could only help. "What about that?" Again, to my surprise, she gave a little nod and left.

Rosie returned four months later with a skin issue, and had, remarkably, lost a few more pounds. I thought to myself, *She's following my advice. She's trying to make a positive change for Rosie. I'm slowly but surely, getting through to her.*

At that visit, I proposed a therapeutic weight-loss diet (high-protein, high-fiber worked best in this case). We were gradually winning the fight against Rosie's obesity. And guess what? She changed Rosie's diet and within six months Rosie achieved her ideal weight of seventy-five pounds. It had taken over a year-and-a-half, but we'd done it, no fuss involved. Rosie's weight loss wasn't the result of a dramatic dietary revolution or an intense exercise program. Rosie lost weight by making small, consistent changes over time. First, we changed her treats, then adjusted portion sizes, then optimized Rosie's nutritional formulation. At the same time, her kids had grown a little older and started taking Rosie outside to play, making Rosie their playmate. I'm certain that if Rosie hadn't lost the excess weight and regained her vitality, she would not have been able to transform into the children's companion. Because Rosie had transformed her body and spirit through weight loss, she was ready, and able, to be their best friend. She could now chase balls, roam parks, and create memories that only humans and dogs can make.

Rosie and her family taught me the importance of patience. Real health and fitness are not about looking good for the upcoming bikini season, but how you'll feel and what you'll be able to do over the next few decades. Dogs such as Rosie will live a long time (Rosie lived to be thirteen) and we need to make sure they are as happy, fit, and as physically able as possible. What if Rosie's playmates had grown up without developing a deep human-animal bond? How would that have affected their development and future? My responsibility was to care for Rosie, but I believe my actions positively impacted the children and entire family. What if nothing had changed and this family had continued to live with a morbidly obese golden retriever? How would the children react when Rosie eventually couldn't walk due to obesity and had to be euthanized at age nine instead of becoming a full, vibrant, and interactive part of the family? It's a dog's life but something much bigger is at stake. I believe our pet's quality of life affects our own.

HAPPINESS WITH YOUR DOG

Better You, Better Dog, Better Life. The title of this book could not be more important. Not only will healthy nutrition enhance your dog's weight and quality of life, it will also help you to eat healthier foods. That's a better you. I've often noticed that clients who have taken better nutrition for their dog seriously, begin to improve their own wellness. Feeding your dog nourishing foods often transfers to your own eating habits. After all, the nutritional requirements of dogs and humans are not all that different. Dogs and humans are classified as omnivores. Both of us need a balanced diet consisting of nutrients available in a wide variety of food sources. Feeding your dog healthier food raises your awareness of food and health. As you embark on a mission to improve your dog's quality of life, your health and vitality will benefit, if you let it.

For me, this journey is really about finding meaning and happiness. Research proves that people who own pets are generally happier than those who don't [10]. Your dog enriches your life through a variety of physiological and psychological mechanisms. If you see your dog is healthy and happy, this state has the potential to positively influence your own well-being. Other scientific studies demonstrate that the mere physical presence of a dog can lower your blood pressure. Petting a dog has been shown to reduce stress.

Living with a pet may also reduce loneliness and depression. Pet owners report talking with and confiding in their dog or cat. Pets may not understand exactly what we are saying, but they listen. And through listening, a special form of intimacy is forged. Your dog is your companion, and you owe it to him or her to nurture that richness through love, which definitely includes good nutrition as well as physical activity, which David covers in Week Three.

WHAT DO I FEED MY OWN DOGS?

I imagine by now you're wondering about my own pets. My dog Sandy is a sixteen-year-old "beach mutt." She has sandy hair, of course, that is shading gray these days. Although she doesn't have the stamina she did when younger, she's always been a fantastic runner and still accompanies me on shorter, slower runs. Sandy is an important part of our family, having helped raise our two daughters. She's a great protector and caregiver. Thanks to years of a healthy diet and exercise, she is lean and strong, sinewy, and agile.

Harry, a busy Border terrier, is six years old. I received him from one of my veterinary colleagues. I like to joke that due to his British heritage, Harry takes no prisoners and knows no enemies. Although he's not an especially good long-distance runner, he's a brisk walker and loves to swim. Harry makes up for his lack of endurance with abundant affection. If he sees an open lap, he's going to be in it, maybe a lot like your dog.

The next question, I can hear you thinking, "What do you

feed your dogs, Dr. Ernie? And do they really eat vegetables?" Those are great questions. The short answers are, 1) A Hybrid Menu, and 2) Absolutely. Now for the slightly longer explanations.

When it comes to regular meals, I feed my dogs what I've termed the Hybrid Menu. Nearly twenty years ago, I was struggling with finding what I believed to be the most wholesome and nutritious diet for my dogs. Was it a commercial product in a bag or can or a home-prepared meal with fresh, whole foods? I found that a combination of the two was ideal. I would cook for my pets whenever time permitted, usually on the weekends. I would refrigerate or freeze these meals for use during busy weeknights. When I ran out of home-cooked food, I'd feed the best commercial dog food I could find. In general, I'd feed two to four home-prepared meals, and three to five commercial feedings per week. Once I gained confidence with this approach with my own pets, I began recommending it to my veterinary patients. I preferred the Hybrid Menu, adding top-quality dog food. This lessened the concern over the exact micronutrients in home-cooked meals as long as the commercial diet was half or more of the total diet. The Hybrid Menu allowed me to focus on feeding real, whole foods containing essential, unaltered nutrients that processed kibble may lack. I encourage you to consider a Hybrid Menu approach and at least try adding real, fresh foods to dry or canned pet food whenever possible to optimize health and promote food satisfaction.

As for feeding vegetables as dog treats, it's a lot easier than you might guess. Some dogs like softer textures and some like crunchy. Some dogs wish for warm vegetables, others prefer them at room temperature, while a few prefer their veggies crispy and cool. Don't be afraid to experiment. I regularly feed my dogs broccoli, cucumber, zucchini, celery, and asparagus.

I frequently add sweet potatoes to dry kibble when pressed for time. My dogs are served portions of our morning vegetable-and-fruit smoothie nearly every day. (Yes, we have to clean Harry's Border terrier beard afterwards.) Try substituting processed dog treats with real foods. Your dog's health will thank you.

HOW DOES NUTRITION INTERSECT WITH FITNESS?

I want to be clear: the journey toward optimal health is not always easy. Nutrition alone will not yield the best results. You cannot achieve optimal health for your pet (or yourself) without daily physical activity. In Week Three, David will expertly guide you on how to achieve fitness with your pet through simple activities. My role is to emphasize the need for both nutrition and movement as being necessary for lasting health, vitality, and disease prevention. Of course, everyone wants a simple answer to health and longevity: "It's the diet!" some would say. "It's genetics!" proclaim others. "It's the owners!" many argue. But, it's not that simple. Weight loss and optimal health are much more than exercising more or eating less. It's the simultaneous combination of many efforts that create your and your dog's best life.

According to the Centers for Disease Control and Prevention (CDC), "You gain weight when the calories you burn, including those burned during physical activity, are less than the calories you eat or drink" [11]. It's important to have a rough idea of how much you are eating and of how many calories you are burning. The CDC recommends working your way up to 150 minutes per week of moderate-intensity aerobic activity or 75 minutes per week of vigorous intensity activity, or a mix of the two [11]. The CDC further states that "Strong scientific evidence shows that physical activity can help you maintain your weight over time" [11]. The CDC also points out that these results vary from person to person.

All dogs need daily aerobic exercise, exercise that gets the heart pumping, lymphatics draining, and cellular mechanisms firing. When your pet exercises, many positive things result. Exercise boosts the immune system, builds strong bones, joints, and tendons, strengthens muscles, and enhances heart and lymphatic function. In essence, exercise boosts your and your dog's well-being. It's unfortunate, but in addition to an epidemic of pet obesity, we have an epidemic of inactivity in our dogs. A dog that is largely inactive is going to develop medical and behavioral conditions that could have been prevented. We must consciously combine the concept of nutrition with fitness to achieve wellness.

There are three degrees of health I consider: 1) ill, 2) healthy, and 3) optimal wellness. Most physicians and veterinarians focus on the ill/healthy divide. Healthy is thought of as the absence of illness. I don't see it that way. Healthy is definitely better than illness, but we should strive for another state of being: optimal health. I define the optimal health state as achieving an individual's or pet's full potential for strength, stamina, creativity, intelligence, and purpose. Humans want to enjoy life to the fullest, and we should pursue that for our pets as well. If I simply limit my veterinary practice to treating illness, then I omit disease prevention. If I focus solely on preventive medicine, then I may overlook the pursuit of optimal health. The best physicians and veterinarians understand this and strive to attain optimal health for each patient.

How do you know if you reach optimal health? How do you know if your pet is fully well? Think back to your childhood or your dog's puppyhood. Optimal health is a feeling of confidence, security, energy, ambition, contentment, joy, and strength generally associated with youth. In addition to those attributes, optimal health also means you have a finely tuned sense of physical awareness, you understand (and control) your emotions and actions and possess clarity in thought. I guarantee you'll know it when it happens. Maintaining this state requires daily effort and paying close attention to dietary details and daily habits. I personally find I experience periods of weeks where I achieve this elevated state almost effortlessly, but then travel or a life event interferes, and I must start over. You should never be satisfied with your current state of health or that of your dog, but be patient. The goal should be to make every day, month, year or decade better than the previous one.

WHAT IS THE IMPACT OF HYDRATION ON DOG FITNESS?

Nutrition is a keystone of health, but we also have to consider hydration. Fortunately, dogs are excellent exercisers due to their biology and physiological adaptations. Dogs do not perspire like humans, so they lose less water than a human through sweating. We must factor in hydration not only during exercise, but as a factor in optimal health. Duration, temperature, and humidity are important variables when calculating how much water your dog needs during exercise. The longer the exercise, the hotter the temperature, and the higher the humidity, the greater the need for your pet to drink. Even for an out-of-shape dog, going outside for thirty minutes is fine, no water required except for in the hottest, most humid conditions. If you and your pet are outside exercising beyond thirty minutes, it's above eighty-five degrees or 80 percent humidity, then bring water with you. Staying hydrated is part of being healthy. If your dog is peeing and the urine is a clear, golden yellow, that is a good sign of proper hydration. If the urine is bright yellow, has a strong odor, or if your dog is urinating small amounts, then play it safe and give more water. Just a note, as diabetes is a common consequence of obesity in pets, scant, foul-smelling, and frequent urination and increased water consumption could be signs your dog is developing diabetes.

HOW MUCH SHOULD MY DOG WEIGH?

This is one of the most common questions that I receive from dog owners. Your veterinarian will perform a Body Condition Score (BCS) to help determine your pet's current physical condition and ideal weight. I use a BCS Scale of 1 to 9 to help explain a pet's body condition:

Body Condition Score	Description
1	Underweight—Ribs, spine, hips, and other boney prominences easily visible from a distance. No obvious body fat and significant loss of muscle mass
2	Underweight—Ribs, spine, hips, easily visible. Other boney prominences may be seen. No palpable body fat and minimal loss of muscle mass.
3	Healthy Thin—Ribs easy to palpate with no fat covering them. Tops of spines visible. Hip bones may be visible. Obvious waist and abdomen is tucked and sloped upward.
4	Ideal—Ribs easily palpable with minimal fat covering. Waist observed from above. Abdominal tuck present.

5	Ideal—Ribs easily felt without excessive fat covering. Waist observed from above. Abdominal tuck present.
6	Overweight—Ribs easily felt but with fat covering present. Waist is observed but not prominent. Abdominal tuck present.
7	Overweight—Ribs able to be felt with difficulty, with heavy fat cover. Fat deposits over lower back and base of tail. Waist not observed or barely present. Abdominal tuck may not be present.
8	Obesity—Unable to feel ribs, except with significant pressure. Heavy fat cover over ribs and spines. No waist or abdominal tuck. Obvious abdominal enlargement.
9	Obesity—Significant fat deposits over chest, spine, hips, and base of tail. Waist and abdominal, tuck absent. Fat deposits along neck and legs. Obvious abdominal enlargement.

I've also included a chart that shows desired weight ranges by breed in Appendix Two.

In addition to the BCS and breed weight charts, here are the five basic steps I perform to assess a dog's weight: 1) viewing the dog from the side, 2) viewing the dog from the rear, 3) viewing the dog from above, 4) feeling the dog, and 5) calculating the pet's BCS.

First, with your dog standing, step back and look at her from the side. What do you see? What you don't want to see are rolls of fat, a chunky neck and shoulders (compared to head size), a stomach that hangs lower or is wider than the chest, a forward slope with too much weight on the front legs, and skinny legs supporting the torso. Ideally, what you see is a lean torso with the chest wider than the stomach on legs that seem proportional to the rest of the body.

Second, examine your dog from the rear. Does your dog look too wide for her legs? The chest and stomach of overweight dogs will bulge. Your dog should have that streamlined look and not look like a plump hotdog on a stick.

Third, view your dog from above, going from front to back. Look for a neck that is too wide for the head (keep in mind some breeds, such as pit bulls and bulldogs, have a wide, short neck). Also, does the chest seem too wide for the head? A small head paired with a broad, bulbous body suggests too much fat. Can you see a clearly defined waist, or is it just one mass that gets wider from shoulders to hips, like a torpedo or blimp? Having a wide, bulging belly indicates that there is too much abdominal fat, the most potentially dangerous and biologically active form of adipose tissue.

Fourth, feel your pet's chest, mid-section, and hips. Ideally you can see the outline of three or four ribs, but you should certainly be able to feel all of them and count them. If you feel a roll of fat instead, this is one of the easiest ways to tell your pet may be overweight or has obesity. Next, feel for the shoulder blades, which you should be able to detect with slight pressure. How about the stomach? Is the belly loose and sagging or thin and tight? Palpating your dog's spine is like feeling along the ribs. Walk your fingers down the dog's back feeling for each vertebra, which should be distinct and not hidden beneath a layer of fat. Finally, check the hip bones, which you should be able to easily feel without applying significant pressure.

Last, calculate your dog's body condition score (BCS) using the chart on pages 65-66. Ideally your pet is lean and muscular. You do not want your dog to appear emaciated or excessively thin, or obese and physically limited, but to be a lean, functionally strong body condition. Ultimately, you want to bring your dog into the category of "Ideal" with a BCS of 4–5 on a 1–9 scale. There is no quick fix for achieving an ideal body condition score, but following the guidelines presented in this book will help you succeed. Remember that your dog loves you unconditionally and wants to please you. She's also depending on you to make healthy decisions for you both. Feeding your dog more and offering more treats will not make her love you more.

It's also important to note that your dog may develop obesity due to a medical condition, which your veterinarian can diagnose and treat. The most common disease that creates overweight and obesity is hypothyroidism, or low thyroid hormone production. I always eliminate diseases such as hypothyroidism before beginning any weight-loss or exercise program. Another disease that can contribute to excess weight is Cushing's disease, which results in the release of excess cortisol. An increased appetite is one of the signs of Cushing's disease. There are also other factors that can lead to overweight and obesity, including stress, arthritis, respiratory conditions, heart disease, ascites (swollen belly), viruses, and intestinal microorganisms. Genetics and environmental toxins may also play important roles in the development of obesity. Certain medications may also lead to excess weight such as the anti-seizure medication phenobarbital and corticosteroids used to treat allergies and immune-related diseases. Regardless of the exact cause or contributing factors, I believe it's critical we accept obesity as a disease and treat it as such.

FEEDING YOUR DOG

Let's revisit what's important to feed your dog. To reduce

weight, I typically begin with a high-protein, high-fiber, low-carbohydrate diet. If you have ever dieted, you recognize this mantra among many of the human weight-loss programs out there such as the South Beach Diet, Paleo Diet, or Atkins Approach. High protein, low carbs: That's what our current understanding of the research tells us will most reliably aid in canine weight loss.

In simplest terms, when you reduce caloric intake, your body is forced to find calories within itself. The risk is that some of those calories will come from healthy muscle, a condition we want to avoid when losing weight. Higher protein diets have been proven to help preserve lean muscle mass during weight loss. Another beneficial attribute of dietary protein is that it tastes good and is very filling. Your dog will feel fuller and for longer. By feeding a high-protein weight-loss diet, you'll find your dog will pester you less for treats and extra meals, which will make your job easier.

I've talked about the value of fresh foods for your dog, and for yourself, but what about commercial dog foods? I've mentioned that I feed my dogs both home-prepared and commercial foods. When it comes to choosing a dog-food brand, you need to do a little investigation. The good news is that commercial dog foods available in the United States, Canada, United Kingdom, European Union, Australia, and New Zealand are generally complete and balanced and safe. I'm always worried about pet food contamination, but I've come to realize that government regulators do an excellent job keeping our food sources as safe as possible.

The biggest danger with commercial or home-prepared pet food is that you will feed too much. It's very important to precisely measure the portions and weighing them is even better. In Appendix Three, you'll find a chart that will help you portion your dog's food according to its target weight.

THE HYBRID MENU

I advocate a feeding strategy I call the Hybrid Menu. How can you add variety and nutrition into your dog's diet? It's not as hard you think. Of course, you can rely on providing a high-quality, commercial dog food. During this week of "food bowl awareness" that's what you should focus on. The first week of better nutrition is also time to begin thinking about how you can feed your dog even better.

A Hybrid Menu is essentially a combination of high-quality commercial dog food on most days along with two to four days of home-cooked meals. It's not as hard as it sounds. Basically, you cook for yourself and your dog, so you're just adding in a portion to your regular recipes. Of course, this doesn't mean a juicy hamburger with bacon and cheese and fries or triple-cheese pizza but a healthy meal that is wholesome and nourishing.

Here are the basics for home cooking for your dog: Choose a quality protein such as salmon or turkey, preferably organic or wild-caught. Combine that with a grain such as quinoa or brown rice and combine that with superfoods such as sweet potato, minced or chopped spinach, or broccoli. Sound good? Keep reading. This can be a meal you are preparing for both yourself and your dog, so avoid added spices and be stingy with salt. Of course, you can prepare meals specifically for your dog (that's what I do), using less spice and salt than you might prefer, and prepare them ahead of time and freeze them. Many people, especially families with busy schedules, like to pre-make their meals a week in advance and have them ready when time pressure mounts.

You'll be pleasantly surprised to see your dog wolf down these delicious, fresh, home-cooked supplemental meals. The key is portion control. Don't accidentally overfeed your pet simply because they really like it. A good rule of thumb is to look for recipes containing about 200 calories per cup of fresh-cooked food.

What about desserts and treats? You like desserts and so does your dog, but not your usual pecan pie. One of my favorite dessert treats for your dog is simple, low-calorie, and packed with powerful nutrients. Just blend a half cup of blueberries with a half cup of probiotic-rich, plain, non-fat yogurt. No sugar needed.

What are some tips to remember when home-cooking meals for your dog? It may be that your dog doesn't like hot or cold foods. Try serving the meal at room temperature or slightly cold. Vary the menu. No one likes to eat the same meat and veggies over and over. Learn what your dog likes, but also encourage a range of foods and experiment with new ingredients. Pet owners fear adding a new protein, grain, or vegetable will cause intestinal distress. I've found dogs fed a wide variety of foods have fewer gastrointestinal issues than dogs fed only a single commercial food.

One of my favorite proteins for dogs are wild-caught fish. This could be tuna, salmon, or sardines. The omega-3 fatty acids found in oily fishes, DHA and EPA, are especially good for your pet's overall health and add vibrant flavor to the dish. In regard to vegetables, don't overlook the humble sweet potato. Sweet potatoes are an excellent superfood for dogs, rich in fiber and vitamins A and C. If you find your dog is avoiding a particular vegetable, mince it and mix it with the grain and meat. If you still can't get them to eat the dish (which is rare) try adding just a splash of ketchup (the kind without high-fructose corn syrup).

There are some foods that pose potential health risks to your dog. Here is a short list: chocolate, coffee, caffeine, alcoholic beverages, macadamia nuts, grapes and raisins, onions, garlic, chives, rhubarb leaves, foods with xylitol (a sugar-free sweetener found in candy and baked goods), raw or undercooked meat and eggs, and bones. There are potentially many more, so be sure to check with your veterinarian when considering a new food for your dog.

And there you have it, a simple and efficient way to improve your pet's nutrition. Remember to vary your dog's diet to prevent any nutritional deficiencies and focus on feeding high-quality proteins with fewer carbohydrates.

WHAT ARE THE TOP CONSEQUENCES OF A DOG BEING OBESE?

The number one consequence of obesity is a shorter lifespan and decreased quality of life, whether human or dog. You want your dog, and yourself, to live life to the fullest, not only in terms of quantity but also quality. There is ample evidence of obesity causing decreased life expectancy in humans [12, 13] and animals [14, 15]. In landmark lifetime studies, dogs that were fed 25 percent fewer calories lived about 2 years longer. That is a lot to think about. And, it's not just a matter of dying before our time. The dogs in these studies also had lower incidences of arthritis and cancer and higher mobility and quality of life scores than the dogs fed a "normal" amount [14, 15].

Second, osteoarthritis, or crippling arthritis, is one of the most frustrating and debilitating illnesses I see as a veterinarian, and it is directly caused or worsened by obesity. Arthritis and degenerative joint disease (DJD) affects nearly every aspect of a dog's life. Not only is it painful, but there is no cure, other than to surgically replace the diseased joint. It is truly a devastating disorder, requiring lifelong treatment. Many dogs can avoid arthritis and DJD simply by maintaining a healthy weight.

A third consequence of obesity is diabetes. The most common clinical sign of diabetes in dogs (and humans) is excessive thirst and urination. Caring for a pet with diabetes is challenging and can have devastating consequences in terms of a multitude of health complications and poor quality of life.

Fourth on the list is cancer. Obesity in humans and animals increases the risk for many cancers. This is the emerging reality of the obesity and cancer link. The question I get most often is: "How the heck does obesity cause cancer?" There are currently three main mechanisms for obesity leading to cancer. The first and most important way that obesity leads to cancer is that fat cells secrete estrogen and estrogen-like compounds. This can lead most commonly to breast cancer or ovarian cancer. Remember, even if your pet has been spayed or neutered, she or he can still get breast cancer.

Another mechanism of cancer associated with obesity is the secretion of insulin-like growth factor (IGF-1). IGF-1 is secreted by the liver but is also secreted by fat cells. IGF-1 tells the body's cells to divide more rapidly. Every time a cell divides you run the risk of a DNA malfunction, which can cause cancer. The third avenue of cancer via obesity is simply chronic inflammation. When the body produces fat, those fat cells signal inflammation within the immune system. In response to this inflammatory stimulus, a type of white blood cell known as a macrophage releases chemical signaling agents called cytokines. An example of the cytokines secreted includes tumor necrosis factor (TNF).

Models of human obesity can often be translated to our canine friends. Much of the research about human obesity is applicable to dogs. Dogs are most likely to get many of the same cancers that humans develop, such as cancers of the breast, bone, esophagus, stomach, colon, pancreas, and kidney.

So, what about the costs associated with diseases related to obesity? Similar to healthcare for humans, treating a pet with obesity-related disorders is not cheap. Fortunately, we have health insurance plans for pets that I strongly recommend to every pet owner. Let's continue thinking about cancer and the costs that can be incurred. What does cancer treatment look like in animals? As with humans, chemotherapy for pets can be given by mouth or intravenously, but without many of the associated side effects. In dogs, there is usually no loss of hair, minimal to no nausea, and most dog patients do very well, with a noticeable improvement in energy and activity. An important factor to consider when considering cancer treatment is the impact on quality of life. How will your dog be better with chemotherapy? Most dogs can enjoy a high quality of life after successful cancer treatment, but you want to have clear expectations from your veterinarian before pursuing any cancer treatment regimen.

What about the cost for treating cancer? Cancer treatment costs vary wildly from hundreds to thousands of dollars for six to eighteen months of treatment. On average, most courses of chemotherapy or surgery run between $2,000 and $7,000.

What do I see most often in my clinical practice? To be honest, only a minority of the pets I diagnose with cancer receives what I would call "complete cancer therapy" consisting of radical surgery or radiation therapy and/or aggressive chemotherapy. Usually it is a case of "doing nothing" or "everything possible."

I most frequently encounter two treatment scenarios when I diagnose cancer. The first is the owner who has no idea his dog has cancer. Perhaps he brings his dog in because he has stopped eating, lost weight, or is exhibiting some serious symptom, but no obvious growths or masses. The second scenario is an alert owner who realizes that something subtle but serious is happening, although they're not sure exactly what's wrong.

We then have two possible responses from the owners when confronted with a cancer diagnosis. The first is usually pretty clear: cancer equals euthanasia. The dog owner says, "I'm not putting my dog through that," which is unfortunate, but understandable. Many of these pet owners have witnessed a friend or family member struggle through chemo and simply don't want their pet to undergo treatment. Some of these owners also don't have pet insurance or the ability to spend thousands of dollars caring for their pet's disease. The second response finds a pet owner considering how treatment will affect their pet's quality of life. Money isn't the concern; outcomes are. This category, in my experience, is about 10 to 25 percent of the pet owners.

Ultimately, cancer is scary and expensive, but you can help prevent cancer by avoiding obesity. As I often say, "Obesity isn't a problem until it's a catastrophe." Let's change that.

NUTRITION AND THE OLDER DOG

As we age, our body's nutritional needs change. Our metabolic processes shift, and our bodies tend to store fat versus burning it. Ageing also is associated with decreased physical activity due to a normal loss of muscle tissues. In Week Three, David provides valuable information on physical activity and the older dog, but here we'll focus on nutrition, especially on minimizing weight gain.

Weight management is an important aspect of physical therapy in older dogs, especially those with orthopedic and neurological problems. Excess weight contributes to the development of musculoskeletal diseases and places excessive strain on joints, tendons, and ligaments, thus aggravating existing health problems. Consequently, effective weight management is an extremely important factor in the success of physical therapy in older dogs. The two main target groups are: 1) normal-weight dogs with restricted physical activity, where the goal is *weight maintenance* and 2) overweight pets and those with obesity, where the goal is *weight reduction*.

Energy requirements decrease with age (in dogs at around five to seven years in large breeds and eight to ten years in smaller breeds) and with decreased physical activity. If your pet has been "fixed" (neutered or spayed), their energy requirements are about 20 to 30 percent less than intact animals. The breed of your dog can also affect energy requirements and obesity risk. Certain dogs (e.g., Cocker Spaniels, Labradors, beagles, and golden retrievers) appear to have a genetic predisposition to obesity. Finally, your dog's temperament plays a role in maintaining a healthy body condition. Some dogs are feisty and active, and some dogs are laid-back and prone to lie around.

Energy requirements can vary greatly, even among healthy animals. In animals with reduced physical activity or exercise restriction, calories must be reduced to ensure they do not gain excess weight and fat. We also must consider environmental conditions such as climate and any underlying diseases that your dog may have such as hypothyroidism, which dramatically affects metabolism and conversion of calories to fat. Ultimately, the amount of food given to your older dog should be adjusted to maintain his ideal weight and body condition. If you have doubts about how much to feed, your veterinarian is your best resource.

What is a good weight-management strategy for the older dog? Animals with long-term exercise restrictions due to medical reasons will have decreased energy requirements. It is important in these pets to develop a weight-maintenance plan based on a nutritious, low-calorie diet. The evidence for weight loss in older dogs also points to higher-protein, low-carb diets.

Treats must be accounted for in feeding, which, as we've discussed, can be a real problem for some pet owners. For each treat the pet receives during the day, its food must be reduced accordingly. Treats may consist of commercial, light, or diet snacks as well as low-calorie fruits and vegetables (e.g., apples and carrots). In general terms, treats should never exceed 10 percent of your dog's total daily calorie allowance. If treats are fed in excess, we risk causing weight gain and nutritional deficiencies. In addition, an older pet should be weighed at least every three months, to identify weight gain early as possible.

Of course, as David and Tricia will agree, I encourage you to engage in activities with your older pet several times daily. Massage and movement exercises, such as gently flexing your senior dog's legs, are two excellent examples of activities that are both pleasant and beneficial. However, they do not have a significant impact on energy expenditure. But this simple activity will have a positive effect on your dog's musculoskeletal system and his sense of well-being and also gives you a better feeling about imposing the dietary restrictions. After all, we have our pet's best interests in mind.

STAYING MOTIVATED

I avoid using fear to motivate pet owners (or humans) to pursue optimal health. I find little value in trying to scare or shame someone into action. The decision for positive change needs to come from a positive perspective. As a veterinarian, I discuss the potential (and often frightening) consequences of obesity, but fear is not my focus. My focus is on what is best for your dog, what can help your dog achieve optimal health, and how you can preserve and prolong the bond you share with your dog.

The tendency when receiving bad news is to distance yourself from that bad news. Informing a pet owner that their dog has obesity can make them feel guilty, that they are somehow not being a good pet parent and harming their dog. As a caring veterinarian, I share medical facts and figures, health risks, and rewards, but my most important role is to be supportive and reframe the problem in terms a pet owner can relate to. When I see a dog with obesity, I see disease and chronic inflammation. I want to put the owner in charge of their pet's health versus an order from a doctor. I strive to empower each and every pet owner to make positive change in their pet's life.

Ultimately, how does obesity make this animal feel? To discover this, I try to imagine that I'm the pet patient. Am I feeling more tired? Do I have less energy? Do I have the motivation or desire to play fetch or go for a walk? I try to really dig into the emotional and psychological state of the dog as well as treating the biological disease.

An often-unappreciated role of a veterinarian is to be an interpreter for your dog. My job is to be the voice of the pets I serve, explaining to owners what and why their pet needs something. How does obesity impact the dog, and how is this medical condition affecting the human family? I want the owner to think, "How does my dog feel today? How can she feel better?" If you, the owner, say, "He feels sluggish and his joints are achy" then that is a first step to improvement.

Tricia, David, and I are not here to merely dispense advice. We are here to empower you to take action with your and your dog's best interest in mind. You are caring for a living and loving being. As with human children, you are making the decision of better health for them. I'm here to guide you, provide information and offer support. It's also critical for you to build a local community of support around you and your dog. All too often, if you act alone, you'll only be able to sustain your efforts for a short period of time. To improve your chance of success, it is important to become part of an extended, like-minded, supportive community. You will read more about the importance of community in Week Four. What matters most now is that we continue on this journey toward better health, to develop the habits needed to succeed, and for the three of us to encourage and cheer you on.

As a further motivation, I have found that many pet owners transfer their newfound pet nutritional wellness to their own diets. Together, we have raised an awareness of how better nutrition results in a healthier dog and a healthier you. You are the most important component of your dog feeling better and obtaining optimal health, and that healthy energy can spread into your own life.

WILL GOOD NUTRITION MAKE MY DOG SMARTER?

The short answer is yes, and there is data to prove it. As David will share in Week Three, physical activity and games also sharpen a dog's brain function. A dog that sleeps all day and receives little interaction will soon become a dull pet. An overweight dog or dog with obesity fed an excessive amount of unhealthy foods will decline in mental sharpness. In other words, regular exercise and healthy foods have been shown to help preserve mental abilities in dogs and humans. There are even therapeutic dog foods containing medium-chain triglycerides (MCTs) that claim to boost your dog's mental abilities. I encourage you to explore these exciting nutritional advances, especially if your dog is older or experiencing decline in brain function. We can help our dogs stay mentally sharp by providing good nutrition that supports their memory and mental agility.

There are a variety of causes of mental decline in dogs, including reduced brain mass and a reduction in neurons [16]. Quoting Bill Milgram, Kane notes, "Most dramatically, older dogs lose their ability to learn..." [16]. This occurs gradually, and unnoticed at first, but it's never too late to intervene and give your dog the best brain health possible. You may notice your dog begins to soil the house, reduces her level of activity, seems disoriented and wanders, and interacts less with humans and other pets as signs of mental decline [16].

One key ingredient of dog foods designed to improve brain function are antioxidants. According to Kane, "Researchers [have] hypothesized that dietary intervention could help combat free radicals and the effect of oxidative stress on the ageing brain" [16]. Basically, an antioxidant inhibits the oxidation of various molecules, which can create physiological stress within the brain and may directly damage brain tissues. Antioxidants include the fat-soluble vitamins A, D, and E, and MCTs. In a study with older beagles, Pan and colleagues say this: "The MCT-supplemented group showed significantly better [mental] performance in most of the test protocols than the control group" [17]. This is exciting research with tremendous promise to help older dogs age more gracefully.

It's true that antioxidants and MCTs may improve mental function, but the best results occur, as David and Tricia will concur, when combined with daily physical activity. There is no magic pill to boost your pet's brain power (yet), and it requires some effort on your part to provide that extra help that your best friend needs. As always, if you have any questions about the best dog food for your pet or supplements, given its weight, age, condition, and overall nutritional status, just ask your veterinarian.

BETTER NUTRITION BETTER LIFE

So, take my word. Eating healthier is a worthy goal for you and your dog. Both of you will feel better and will have more energy and drive to engage in the physical activity that David will talk about in the next chapter. It's not the simplest task to accomplish, but with guidance, motivation, and a real goal in mind, you and your dog can succeed. Take these first seven days of better nutrition to heart, starting slowly and building toward longer-term goals.

WEEK THREE: PHYSICAL ACTIVITY AND OPTIMAL HEALTH

—Dr. David Levine—

Welcome to your journey to a better life through physical activity with your dog. Notice that I didn't say exercise. It's similar to Ernie not focusing on dieting but rather using the term nutrition. As you'll see in the story I'm about to tell, physical activity not only involves walking or jogging, but also just moving around, going to the mailbox, climbing some stairs, or pushing a lawnmower if you are able.

RAYMOND'S STORY

I know a retired physician, Raymond, who was in his early seventies when we first met. His wife, Rachel, was a doctor too. They owned a picturesque farm in North Georgia that included a charming small lake. He was enjoying an active retirement, taking care of his property and being outside most of the time. One day he had a severe stroke that took away his ability to speak and seriously damaged the right side of his body. Even after rehabilitation he could barely walk more than ten feet with a walker. Raymond had a faithful dog, but it had died the previous year, and he hadn't been ready to get another dog.

Rachel was worried about him when she was at work. Raymond spent the day in bed or just sitting in his recliner while she was gone. She could tell that he was depressed, and she felt guilty about not being there with him during the day. Being doctors, they knew how difficult the recovery from a stroke could be, and his inability to express himself through speech was very frustrating. When she was home, Raymond could be very demanding, asking her to bring him things constantly and lashing out at her.

I had a chance to talk with Rachel at a social and suggested they get another dog, that it might encourage him to do more while she was gone. I knew that the dog would want to go outside and that Raymond would have to go with him. It took about three months of Raymond just getting worse and Rachel herself sinking into depression, but she found a dog, a Cocker Spaniel mix that they named Ralphy. It was a natural process. Raymond couldn't help but take care of Ralphy. He went from being chairbound to using his walker to go outside and then to using a cane. Walking the dog had such a positive impact on his health that he re-entered outpatient rehabilitation to become as fully functional as possible. He also gave speech therapy another try and made great progress as his attitude improved.

Since it was his right side that was affected, I came up with exercises to strengthen the muscles there. For example, he brushed Ralphy with his right hand three times a day, starting at fifteen brushes but eventually doing it one hundred times or more. Putting on Ralphy's collar and leash enhanced the fine movements of his hands. Walking the dog began to improve his balance, and he felt more confident walking with less fear of falling. I also told him to throw a ball for Ralphy with his right hand to help retrain the muscles on that side, and he got better and better at it. It was an inspiration to see Raymond in action, to see him embrace life again. Instead of just thinking about himself, he had Ralphy to feed and walk. Just petting the dog was good for him and made his recovery more meaningful.

Now Raymond has a mission, taking care of the dog, getting out and walking more, gaining the confidence to go to the grocery store, and walking around his property. This led to him eating better and taking an interest in his overall health. This not only provided more social interaction, but also a better relationship with his wife. Raymond is the first to admit that Ralphy enhanced the quality of his life. Every time I talk to Rachel she says, "You were right." And now, when I drive past their farm, I often see Raymond outside walking with Ralphy. He even has a garden, something he had badly wanted to return to doing in his retirement.

THE FIRST SEVEN DAYS OF BETTER PHYSICAL ACTIVITY

I'm a physical therapist who works with both dogs and people, so I am especially interested in how the two interact. To get started on your journey to better health through being physically active, we need to get a baseline measure of your and your dog's health. Every physical activity program has to be individualized and then coordinated between you and your dog. Typically, a dog will have much better aerobic capacity than a human, so it may be that you have to start much slower than your dog. Make sure that you build in plenty of breaks for you and your dog to rest, until you are able to be continuously active for longer periods of time.

I do recommend that you have a wellness checkup with your doctor and also get a check-up for your dog. We want to make sure that there are not any medical issues that might be complicated by increasing your or your dog's activity levels. This will also be a good time to ask your vet about dietary considerations, to determine how your dog's nutritional needs might change. In Week Two, Ernie has done a great job of explaining your dog's nutritional needs, but it never hurts to ask your vet as well. Another consideration before you get started is equipment you may need for yourself or your dog. If you plan to walk or hike with your dog, you will need sturdy shoes for yourself and a leash and collar or harness for your dog. Avoid use of retractable leashes during physical activity, as they allow the dog to wander and lose focus.

Next, scope out an area where you want to take your dog for your joint activity. The easiest option is to walk out your front door and begin by walking around your neighborhood. Avoid busy streets that do not have sidewalks. Also, take along a poop bag in case your dog just has to go. It happens! It could be that your neighborhood is not walking friendly. In that case, locate a park or area with sidewalks that you can freely use. Tricia started walking with her dog at a nearby football stadium, where she took advantage of the many stairs there. Trails are another good option, but just make sure that you don't get lost. If you plan on walking or hiking for more than thirty minutes, bring some water for yourself and your dog. Pet stores sell collapsible water bowls that are easy to carry. When you increase your time out to perhaps thirty minutes or more, you can also bring along small healthy treats for the two of you. Not that you have to be out for that long. Do what feels right, monitoring your heart rate and the general condition of the dog. If you or your dog become out of breath, slow down or rest. Small dogs have more trouble keeping up than large dogs as they have to take many more steps per minute.

So, how do you go about crafting an activity schedule for you and your dog, especially during this first week of physical activity? It's important that you be reasonable and take it slow. You don't want to injure yourself or your dog, and you don't want to frustrate yourself by overdoing it. If you or your dog is overweight or obese, you should start even slower than what

I'm about to recommend.

So, day one, and you're ready to start! Perhaps you choose a cooler part of the day, the morning or evening, especially if it is summer. If you have a heavily furred pooch, such as a St. Bernard or a chow, you want to be mindful of not overheating the dog. If you do have a really furry dog, you could consider having them get a summer cut to remove the excess coat, unless you live in a colder climate or it's winter. Dogs like bulldogs and pugs have flatter faces that make them more susceptible to breathing problems and heat-related problems.

Let's start with just ten minutes of walking. Leash up the dog and walk outside. You are on a journey, remember that, and this is just the beginning. Ten minutes could be as simple as walking around the block three times. Take it slow and monitor how breathless you and your dog are. Talk to your buddy and praise her as you walk. After ten minutes are you or your dog winded? If so, then you are done for the day. Don't be discouraged that you're starting with what might seem to be small steps. Succeeding with small steps is what will give you the confidence to succeed with the bigger steps.

Motivation is key here. Tricia, Ernie, and I have your best interest at heart, but you'll need that spark that keeps you going from day to day. Ideally, you let others know what you are up to, that you've begun a journey to become healthier and more active. Let others praise you and encourage you. Don't listen to the naysayers who may not be as excited as you are about walking with your dog. If you do get discouraged, don't worry. Come back to this book and re-read some of the passages or visit our website at www.betteryoubetterdog.com for some encouraging tips.

Take the opportunity to praise your dog on your walks. Your dog doesn't need a snack to be rewarded and may actually enjoy a pat on the head and encouraging words much more than a treat. To reward yourself, focus on the dog and the progress she is making. Know that she feels better using her muscles, heart, and brain. She appreciates you and gives you the opportunity to appreciate her.

You just want to stay motivated, as Tricia would say. The last chapter of this book, Week Four—Building Community, will show you how to surround yourself with people who want the best for you. We all need cheerleaders to help us through the dull times as well as the good times. You may feel at times that you are not making progress. If that is the case, pay close attention to the little details. Check your pulse in the middle of a walk for thirty seconds and then multiply by two. Ideally, your heart will be working a little harder. An increase in pulse rate is a good thing. It shows that you are making an effort. If your heart rate is getting beyond 140 beats per minute, slow down. Over time, your maximum heart rate should decrease as you become more fit. Also, pay attention to sweating. Do you break a sweat? This is a sign that your body is responding to the exercise. Take heart in the little things.

Also, pay attention to your dog. Don't let the focus be entirely on you. Notice how curious your dog is on your walks. Believe me, she is having a good time. Like yourself, though, you don't want to press her too hard. Panting is normal for a dog, but you don't want your friend to hyperventilate. If your dog decides to lie down, it could be that she is becoming overheated. Take a break in the shade, but know that her heart is getting stronger, just like yours. You're both making progress, and that's a great thing.

What about your dog's age? Will that make a difference in how you approach your outings with your dog? Of course, but in simple ways that are easily noticeable. Puppies are going to be much harder to control and to keep interested during a simple straightforward walk. Before you walk with your puppy, play with her in the house and get her just a little bit tired. Or start with a brisker pace to tire her and then move into something more comfortable. Don't be discouraged, though, by your puppy's wandering attention. Let her explore on occasion as you walk.

Older dogs will be more likely to fall into step with you as you walk, but still will want to stop and smell the roses. Build in breaks, cued by your dog's behavior, to let her sniff around and check what Ernie calls pee-mail. Where you walk will most likely have been visited by other dogs, and this is of great interest to your friend. Scent marking is an instinctual behavior in which a dog deposits his own odor in the form of urine or feces onto his environment to mark his territory or make a statement. Other dogs who come upon the scent can learn a lot about fellow dogs who have been there. Over time, you'll begin to recognize each other's needs and adapt. Dogs are incredibly smart and are learning as much about you as you are about them.

So, during this first week of activity with your dog, establish a routine. Go for walks at the same time each day if you can, keeping the same distance for this first week. Don't overdo it, as this will discourage you and your dog. But, be flexible as needed. This first week is a time of getting to know your and your dog's initial limitations. Enjoy it, knowing that you will build on your walks and play as time goes by.

Walking with your dog is a bonding experience. The dog-human bond is a powerful relationship, and your dog is going to know that you care even more about her when you take her out for walks. Use the opportunity to teach your dog new commands. Teach her how to sit when you are tired. A dog is very adaptable and will soon learn your limits as well as her own. For encouragement, know that your bond with your pet is strengthened with every outing. It's a mutually beneficial relationship. You will need to take the lead in the relationship, but your dog will follow and give back as much as you put forward. Next, we have Jason's story.

JASON'S STORY

It's not only the elderly who can benefit from caring for a dog. Let me tell you a story about Jason. Jason was twelve and had a severe form of Crohn's disease that caused him abdominal pain, severe diarrhea, fatigue, weight loss, and even malnutrition. He had retreated into a state of anxiety and depression that made it difficult for him to function at home and at school. To make things worse, he was overweight and headed toward type II diabetes. It took us a while, but Jason made what seems to be a miraculous recovery. His anxiety and depression decreased and his self-esteem went through the roof.

Key to his recovery was the addition of an Australian shepherd, Yancy, to his life. Not only did his family adopt Yancy from a shelter, but they began to volunteer at the shelter, which gave Jason confidence and allowed him to make new friends. With Yancy, Jason had a friend to care for and exercise with. Australian shepherds are extremely active and need lots of play time, which was perfect for Jason. With Yancy to look after and to keep up with, Jason had no choice but to strive to be healthier, more open, and more active for the sake of Yancy.

Jason started off slow, just playing with Yancy in the yard. He loved the way that Yancy would run circles around him and nibble at his heels as if he was a sheep. With his mom, Jason began to walk Yancy around the neighborhood, barely able to hold Yancy back. Yancy wanted the exercise as much as Jason needed it. Eventually they wound up walking to a field beside an elementary school and let Yancy run in as big of a circle as she needed, although with her leash trailing behind her. Jason had to run to catch her, and it became a great game between them.

Jason was feeling better, his Crohn's disease less severe it seemed, and he was taking great care of Yancy, who became his best friend. Friends and family alike were amazed at the color that was back in Jason's cheeks and his improved mood. Without Yancy to care for and exercise with, Jason's condition could have worsened, but he was the lucky one when he found Yancy.

YOUR DOG'S ANATOMY

Let's talk a bit about your dog's anatomy and how best to understand your dog's response to exercise. You'll learn a lot just by watching him. You'll learn to monitor his responses to activity just as you will with your own responses. Dogs rely much more on their shoulder muscles than we do. While you are walking on two legs, they are walking on four. They put about 30 percent of their weight on each front leg and about 20 percent on each back leg. It's more of a complete exercise for the dog. Also, dogs are much more efficient aerobic machines than we are and have a better baseline ability for aerobic activity. Just watch for overheating, especially with big furry dogs and flat-faced dogs, and offer water frequently, just like you would drink as you engage in physical activity. Make sure that you are increasing your heart rate within limits but keep it as fun as possible.

PHYSICAL ACTIVITY AND REHABILITATION

What if you are not in the best health? Perhaps you've had a major health problem such as a joint replacement or a heart or lung condition and are involved in rehabilitation or therapy. Of course, you want to listen to what your doctor has to say about your activity. Ask specific questions about what your limits are and follow those guidelines. As I mentioned earlier in the story about Raymond, who had had a stroke, he began slowly, gaining muscle strength and coordination through the simple act of petting and combing his dog. It could be that your first week, or even the first few weeks, have to be focused on getting yourself to the point of even walking around the yard. Just be patient and count the small victories.

Being in rehabilitation is a gradual process, but if you stick with it, you can progress to your body's ideal fitness level. You may have to use a cane or walker, but don't let that slow you down. I do recommend that if you use a cane or walker that your dog be smaller and perhaps older. Older dogs are more patient and less likely to cause a fall. Ideally, if you are reliant on a cane or walker, you have somebody else walk along beside you who can manage the dog. Do not put yourself at risk for further injury. A fall or other accident is the last thing you need.

And, it's just not about physical rehabilitation. Heart disease is the number one killer of persons worldwide. Surviving a heart attack involves cardiac rehabilitation much as a broken hip requires physical rehabilitation. Here again, follow your doctor's or therapist's guidelines. You don't want to compromise yourself by exerting yourself too much and too quickly. Just know that those small steps, those short walks, lead to bigger steps, bringing you closer to your ideal health under the circumstances. If there is a history of cardiovascular disease in your family, now is the time to take action to try and minimize the condition. As always, start slow, but know that activity with your dog could be the key to giving yourself better odds of remaining healthy or at least minimizing the disease process. It's never too late to get started, but always follow your physician's advice.

THE FIRST SEVEN DAYS REVISITED

Let me get back to talking about this being your first week of renewed physical activity with your dog. As with any new venture in which you seek to increase your physical activity, it's a good idea to have an assessment of your baseline health by your doctor, even if you are starting relatively slow, just adding a few minutes at first and taking it easy. As you progress, you will feel that urge to push a little harder. In either case, you should have clearance from your doctor, especially if you have underlying conditions such as heart disease or perhaps suffer from significant excess weight.

Being careful also applies to your dog. If your pet has been relatively inactive or has been diagnosed with a chronic illness, it would be a good idea to have your vet do a physical and recommend some limits. Just remember that this first week is to open the door to the world of active possibilities and not a mad dash to exhaust yourself or your dog. Patience and consistency, with incremental increases in activity as determined by your and your dog's fitness, are essential.

To keep it simple this first week, focus on easy and short walks. Get a feel for how the activity makes you feel. If you are winded, out of breath, or your heart is racing, back off and slow down. Monitor your heart. If it exceeds 140 beats per minute, slow down or rest. This applies to your dog as well. It's harder to check a dog's pulse (there are good online resources to learn how to do this), so watch for labored breathing as a sign that you need to slow down. Choose a part of the day when the sun is not out in full force to minimize stress from the heat.

With any physical activity, it's best to prepare your body for the exertion. This involves two activities, warming up and stretching. You don't have to be a yoga master to do some stretches. But first, warm up by walking through the house or perhaps a round or two in the backyard, slow and easy. If it's cold, wear warm clothes to help your body warm up. If you have stairs, and feel up to it, walk the dog up and down the stairs two or three times.

Now that you've warmed up, some simple stretches are in order. Hopefully, these simple stretches will feel good. If there is any pain, back off. The simplest stretch is to bend over and reach for the floor. Reach as far as you can without straining and hold that position for ten to twenty seconds and repeat five to ten times. If you can touch the floor, great, but if not just give yourself time. This stretch will help loosen up your hamstrings and your Achilles tendon. Another basic stretch is to stand on a step with the balls of your feet and let your weight push your heels down. This is great for stretching your calves. Just let your weight do the work and try to hold the stretch for ten to twenty seconds and repeat five to ten times. Next, limber your upper body by reaching for the ceiling to stretch the muscles beneath your armpits and bend at the waist to loosen your back.

If you want to go the extra step and keep track of your progress, a simple notebook will work. Ernie recommends keeping a log of what you feed your dog and that same principle applies here. Recording your activities acknowledges that you are putting in the effort, and you can watch in amazement as you progress as well as your dog. Write down the simple facts, such as "stretched for five minutes" and then jot down where and how far you walked. Each day read what you wrote the previous day and imagine what the next steps will be, as you reach to attain a comfortable level of activity that leaves you and your dog feeling good.

So, let's say you warmed up by walking with your dog around the backyard twice then stretched for ten minutes. You then headed into the neighborhood for a ten-minute walk. If the activity is new to you and your dog, your heart rate will increase, your body will warm, and you may even break a light sweat, which is great. While you're walking, your dog will want to stop and sniff, or if she's a puppy she may easily become distracted. Ideally, you do a short walk where you let the dog sniff and take in all of the wonderful and some not-so-wonderful smells. Then, after the fun, try and engage her in a steady walk. Initially, treat your walk as a time to be leisurely but not easily disrupted. It may take a few outings, but your dog will get it and learn to walk with minimal distraction.

One tip is to use a relatively short leash (around four feet), one that keeps the dog more or less at your side. You want to walk with the dog versus being pulled or pulling. Frequently praise your friend as you walk and give gentle tugs and voice commands to walk when she gets distracted. You definitely want to avoid getting frustrated and turning what should be pleasurable into a chore. It won't be perfect at first. Just be patient and consistent and always ready with praise.

Once you're back in the house, look forward to a cooling down period, especially if you've worked up a sweat. Have a cool drink (water is always best) and give your dog a nice drink too. Sit in your favorite chair and relive the experience, taking joy in the small steps you are taking. This is another good time to praise your dog for being such a good partner and is the perfect time to record your activity in your notebook. If you're up for it, and are trying to lose some weight, record your weight as well. But don't focus too much on your weight at first. Just let the experience make you feel good and look forward to your next outing with your dog. While on the subject of weight, always weigh yourself first thing in the morning whether it is daily or once a week.

CONTINUING THE JOURNEY

What's next? You've made the leap and committed to an activity plan with your best friend. This is your first week of physical activity, and you're just getting your feet wet, realizing the possibilities. Don't dream too big at first. You don't want to be unrealistic, but now is a good time to set some goals, small steps that you and your dog accomplish together. Let's say that you start off with five minutes of stretching and a ten-minute walk this first week. Start thinking about week two. It may be that you feel like trying fifteen minutes of walking in week two. That's a 50 percent increase in your activity. But, keep your dog in mind, especially if she is overweight. Give yourself and your dog time to build up to more strenuous outings but do set goals that you can achieve and feel good about.

One aspect of your new adventure that we haven't discussed is time. Perhaps you are in pretty good physical shape, but you just don't have time to take your dog for a walk. Life is hectic and demanding, more for some than others, and we all feel the pressure of making time to do what we know is best. Make setting the time aside for activity a goal. If you have to, try and get up a half hour earlier. You don't want to rush yourself and want to leave some cushion time on either side of your walk. It may be that you carve out that extra ten minutes in the morning and then set a goal of making the same commitment for later in the day.

We are all pressed for time it seems. Let's say that you manage the ten minutes in the morning and evening for you and your dog and just can't find more time. In that case, increase the intensity of your minutes. Monitor your pulse and see how quickly you can achieve a rate between 120 and 140. Of course, don't overdo it. If you feel out of breath or dizzy or feel that your heart is racing, slow down. Give your body the time it needs to adjust to the increasing activity as well as your dog's body.

I've touched on this, but here is some simple advice about possibly becoming bored with your initial efforts. Not only can you get bored, but your dog can become bored as well. This probably won't happen in the first week but realize the possibility. So, what can you do?

Start by changing up your stretching routine. Stretch in a different part of the house or perhaps outside. Also, change up what you wear when you walk your dog. There's no need to spend a lot of money, but perhaps a new pair of walking shoes is a way to reward yourself and excite yourself about your new journey. How about a ball cap or two to keep the sun off your head and shade your eyes? And what about the dog? She probably already wears a collar. I would suggest investing in a few cheap bandanas that you can loosely tie around her neck. Put one on before your walks to add a splash of color and signal to her that it's time for her favorite part of the day, getting outside and taking a walk.

Ideally, you are able to create different routes that you take in your neighborhood. Even if you only have one option, perhaps a circular route, do the route in reverse every other day. As you progress, you will find that driving to a walking route may become a possibility if you have the time and resources. Parks and school walking tracks, where dogs are allowed, are ideal to break up the routine. As you set your goals higher, the idea of heading out onto area trails may become an option. Most larger cities have hiking guides. Do some reading, look at some maps, and break up your regular walks with special walks, even if they are short in nature. Most dogs love to ride in cars and that alone may make the outing fun. In Week Four—Building Community, we'll talk about making your walks a social exercise at times. There are lots of people just like you who need to get outside and get active and may be willing to share their walks with you. There is not a simple cookbook approach here, and everyone's tastes are just a little bit different.

MIX IT UP TO STAY ON TRACK

Are there other activities that you can do with your dog? Of course. This first week is all about getting motivated and starting a routine, but you can begin right away, if you choose, to add some spice to the walking routine. If you have stairs in the house, walk with your dog up and down the stairs. It could be that once is enough at first. Perhaps you have a few steps that lead up to your front door or back door. On a short leash, lead your dog down the steps turn and then head back up. Try and do three sets at first. This is a great cardiovascular exercise and develops coordination and balance for both you and your dog. If you do climb stairs, make sure that there is a handrail for you to grab or hold onto should you need it.

But, just know that you have committed to something good, something very good and imagine the possibilities. We've already discussed the idea of taking hikes or going for longer walks. You may even develop to the point that you will want to consider jogging with your dog. We'll talk more about that later. Meanwhile, though, just make it through this first week, accomplishing the goals that you set for yourself. As suggested, keep track of your progress in a notebook, which is a small reward within itself. And here is another simple way to break the routine. Buy a Frisbee or tennis ball for your dog. Spend a few minutes each day playing fetch, perhaps using that time as part of your warm-up for your walks. Or, maybe save the game for later in the day as a reward for the both of you. Labs are notorious for their love of fetching almost anything, and most dogs, but not all, will get the idea and get a good workout at the same time.

Here, I do have to mention a relatively new venue, special gyms for owners and their dogs to exercise indoors. The space is laid out for relays, stepping, and even obstacle courses that you perform with your pet. A great benefit of belonging to such a club is the motivation and camaraderie that is built in. It could be that you live in a small apartment without a yard or a good place to walk in the neighborhood and need an indoor space like a club. It's also a great place to meet other pet lovers just like yourself and share your activity goals with. In Week Four we'll highlight the community building aspect of these dog-human exercise facilities.

MAKING YOUR DOG WALK FUN

We all know that feeling of dread that facing "exercise" can bring. You want to enjoy your walks with your dog, and you need to keep her interested as well. You can begin by pampering yourself and, as suggested, buy a nice pair of walking shoes. If it's in your budget, consider buying an outfit that suits the occasion or wear an old favorite, something that you feel good in. Your dog already knows that picking up the leash means a walk, but how about that special neckerchief for her, maybe different colors on different days?

So, you're ready to venture out and perhaps after a few walks, the routine seems a little lackluster for you and the dog. What follows are some tips from Becker and Kushner to add that extra zip to your dog walks [18].

Your dog loves to be rewarded. You can do this three ways as you walk. First, carry along a healthy snack that your dog likes, keeping in mind the calories you're adding to her diet. At random intervals during the walk ask your dog to sit and surprise her with a treat. If your dog resists the leash, use the treats as a reward for when she picks up the pace and keeps up with you. "Gradually increase the distance from treat to treat, then begin giving treats from your hand as you walk backward. No pulling!" [18] The second way to reward your dog is to "speak your dog's language" [18]. Don't be afraid to get down on the dog's level and slap your thighs in a playful manner for encouragement.

Walks don't have to be continuous. If you have the time, build in a fun activity as you walk. If your dog has a favorite toy bring it along. Try choosing a route that passes by a field or playground where you are welcome to play a quick game but keep your dog on the leash. Sometimes just the sight of the toy is enough to get her attention. Third, talk to your dog as you walk and signal her when she's doing a good job. For good measure give her a good neck scratch.

Another simple trick, according to Becker and Kushner, is to vary your pace. Initially you should try for a steady pace, slow if you have an overweight dog, but pick up the pace on occasion and then slow back down. This will add variety to the walk as you lead the way. My final advice ties in with Week Four—Building Community. Dogs love to be around other dogs. Walking two or more dogs at the same time is a challenge, but you can seek out a friend and walk the dogs together. This makes it more social for you as well as the dog. So, keep it simple, but make it fun.

LOOKING AHEAD

Keeping this first week of physical acctivity in mind, being careful not over-commit and with long-term progress as a goal, let's look ahead just a bit and discuss longer walks and even running, or maybe jogging is the better word. Still key, and even more so, will be the need to plan ahead and warm up.

Let's say you have progressed to walking for twenty minutes twice a day and that you have experimented with ten-minute jogs with a goal to take that up to thirty-minute walks and fifteen-minute jogs. By necessity this means that you are going to be outside longer and need to consider the weather a bit more, how you will dress, and what the dog will need (water if it's hot, a sweater or jacket if it's cold). For thirty-minute walks, it's safe to recommend that your dog will not need water along the way, unless it is very hot and/or humid. Using heat and humidity as a guide and the time you are out, carry water for yourself as well, according to your needs.

First, do your warm-ups and stretch. It may be that you have to stretch from a chair due to advanced age or perhaps an injury, but just make sure that your body is ready for the activity to follow. Where will you walk or run? If you're lucky, maybe you have the option of just heading outside and taking any number of routes. But, it's wise at first to have scoped out your route and to know how long the journey is back home from any point along the way. That way, if you find you need to return early, you'll know the quickest way back. Should you be suffering from a disability, perhaps a bad hip or arthritis, make sure you carry your cell phone with you just in case.

So, let's keep it simple at first, a twenty-minute walk perhaps at a brisk pace, but one that is comfortable for both you and your friend. You've warmed up and stretched and are ready to head out. If you have doubts about your ability, visualize what you are about to do. If you can imagine it, then you can do it. If the entire route seems daunting to you, imagine it in sections. Divide it up and focus on one section at a time. At first, start off slow, maybe letting your pet have a sniff around the mailbox. Keep him on a short leash at your side and with a purpose in mind head toward the first goal of your walk, adjusting your pace as needed. As you walk, talk to your dog, encouraging him.

At the halfway point, give yourself a high-five, and pet your friend, praising him. You'll get a good tail wag and maybe a bark of enthusiasm. Always remember that it's not just you, but that you have someone relying on you to lead the way, even though it may seem that you are being led. You don't want to be overbearing but do keep in mind that you are in control and that the dog is depending on you for guidance and encouragement. Maybe you have one more goal to reach before the final stretch, perhaps the crosswalk at an elementary school. Make a mental note of your accomplishment and keep your forward progress. Within minutes, your house or apartment is in sight, your heart is pumping, and maybe you are breathing deep, but you're not exhausted. You've done it! Your dog has done it, and it's time for a cool down and a round of praise for everyone involved. As you cool down, make a note in your journal about your accomplishment and look forward to your next outing, perhaps that afternoon or the next morning.

Some people ask me if they should feed their dog right after exercising, which seems to make sense. I'll leave it to Ernie in Week Two to provide you with the concrete details, but you should always feed your dog at the same time each day, perhaps twice a day. You should give your dog ample time to eat, but do not leave a full bowl of food all day, encouraging eating around the clock. What I would recommend is to give your dog a healthy snack after an outing, such as a bite of broccoli or a carrot.

YOUR DOG'S BRAIN AND PHYSICAL ACTIVITY

Physical activity such as walking is good for the heart as well as the brain, just like good nutrition. It's especially important as you age that you stay active mentally and physically. It's the same for dogs. According to Pan and colleagues (2010), a dog's brain function is impaired as it ages and mirrors the same decline in humans. Basically, dogs age as we do and experience declines in mental ability as a result. This decline is linked to a function of glucose metabolism in the brain [19].

So, it's important to keep the juices flowing in the brain to try and minimize the overall decrease in glucose metabolism that occurs with age, which is associated with Alzheimer's disease and other disorders. Physical activity is a key part of that strategy. According to researchers, "Regular exercise training slows down age-related brain atrophy" [20]. Physical activity is increasingly recognized as a "low cost, low risk intervention" that protects the brain and restores the central nervous system [20]. Thus, by engaging in physical activity, you are not only protecting yourself and your dog from brain-damaging diseases, you are also restoring brain function that may have already been lost. It's kind of like putting money in the bank and collecting interest. Also, studies indicate that lack of physical inactivity leads to an increased risk for developing dementia [20]. There is no surgery or drugs required, just the effort on your part to incorporate healthy activity into your day and break the cycle of sitting, perhaps taking life a bit too quietly, which is so easy to do. But, with your pet partner, you have an ally and that extra motivation of knowing that you are benefiting not only yourself but another living being that you love and care for and that loves you back for your effort.

WILL EXERCISE MAKE MY DOG SMARTER?

The brain is a complex organ and definitely benefits from exercise. Generally, we refer to cognition, which includes memory, intelligence, and the ability to learn. There is even a field of study called canine cognition, which looks specifically at the brain function of dogs. For thousands of years, dogs have lived closely with humans and have developed an ability to understand and get along with us. Dogs have different learning styles, but dogs raised in close connection with humans are better able to learn commands and respond to human emotions. To join your expectations with your dog's ability to learn, it's important to work on that dog-human bond not just through affection, but also through a healthy lifestyle that includes good nutrition and physical activity. Ernie has already commented on nutrition and the brain, and here we'll look at physical activity.

We've discussed the older dog in terms of the benefits of physical activity, but the older dog's mental state is especially important to consider. According to canine expert Victoria Stillwell, a dog's brain function decreases over time. Changes that you may notice include: "less desire to interact and enjoy activities; abnormally long sleep patterns (particularly throughout the day); toileting accidents in the home; depression and avoidance behavior; sudden appearance of anxiety issues such as separation anxiety and aggression; confusion within a usual environment; and irritability and less tolerance for human touch" [21].

Stillwell's advice on keeping your dog's mental abilities at their best includes activities such as giving your dog puzzles to figure out (for example, hiding a treat), but hinges primarily on physical activity, which includes walking, jogging, and playing. Says Stillwell, "Exercise promotes a feeling of calm and lowers stress both in people and in dogs" [21]. When we, and dogs, exercise, a flood of good chemicals bathes the brain. Most notably, the brain increases levels of neurotransmitters such as serotonin and dopamine, which are key "feel-good" chemicals. Most antidepressants address shortages of these chemicals. So, if your dog seems depressed or lackluster, physical activity is a great way to help him feel better. This is most important with older dogs but applies to younger dogs as well.

Universities such as Yale and Duke now have cognition centers for dogs on their campuses. There are even numerous classes and seminars that you can take with your dog to improve his cognitive ability, usually with exercises that go beyond just your standard walk. Dog-human fitness clubs are a great example. In a specialized dog-human gym, dogs are taken through a variety of exercises such as step exercising and sprints around cones. This works the dog (and you) aerobically, releasing those good brain chemicals, and sharpens the dog's agility, sense of balance, and overall awareness. Plus, there is that special dog-human bond that strengthens. According to dog trainer Sarah Stremming, while discussing her dog Idgie, "I am not sure if she is my spirit animal or if I am hers; but we are a pair and a team each second of each day" [22].

You want to do all that you can to maintain your pet's mental sharpness, and physical activity is key to providing optimal metabolism and increased blood flow to the organs, including the brain, all of which leads to improved brain function. One thing you will want to focus on is communicating with your dog, giving supportive commands and praise while working out. According to researchers, "In direct comparisons, dogs are even more skilled than chimpanzees at using human communicative cues…"[23]. Your dog is smart, some smarter than others, but your pet's brain needs a good workout just as her bones and muscles do. This ability of dogs to understand human speech and gestures is directly tied to their living with us [23]. They have learned over time to adapt and benefit from us and even enjoy and need for us to treat them much as we would an intelligent human friend. In testing for mental differences between dogs with owners and shelter dogs, Hare and his colleagues found that there was no difference in the dogs' abilities to interpret human cues such as pointing. So, don't rule out a shelter dog as a pet because you think it may be less smart, sociable, or trainable.

If you want to test your dog's mental abilities, you can do so with tools such as Dognition, located at www.dognition.com, which involves ten brain exercises. I think you'll be surprised just how smart your dog is. If your dog's profile scores are lower than average they may improve through physical activity and nutrition. One of the interesting exercises involves an owner placing a bowl of food on the floor and telling the dog not to approach the food. The owner then covers his eyes to see how the dog responds [24]. The American Kennel Club (AKC) also provides a range of games to test and improve your dog's brain function. You can find these games at www.akc.org/content/dog-training/articles/fun-cognitive-training-games-for-dogs. According to the AKC, "Mental exercise is just as important as physical exercise for a well-rounded dog. Also, games… strengthen not only your dog's mind, but your bond with your canine companion" [25].

PROTECTIVE EFFECTS OF PHYSICAL ACTIVITY

We've talked about the benefits of physical activity on your brain, but what is the science behind the effects on your body as well? There are two components of walking with your dog that we can consider: the aerobic benefits and what I call the load-bearing benefits.

When you walk, or jog, or take the stairs, your muscles ask for more oxygen and energy. Your body responds in a variety of ways, making more energy available and increasing your heart rate to speed oxygen along to your muscles. A target heart rate of 120 to 140 beats per minute is the ideal upper limit. Beyond that, you should rest and allow your heart rate to slow down. It's difficult to assess your dog's heart rate easily, but you can monitor how heavy the dog is breathing and panting. I have a friend whose dog will just lay down when she is too tired, in the middle of a walk. So, pay attention to yourself and your dog as you walk.

One benefit of encouraging your heart to beat faster is that your resting heart rate should improve, that is, your heart should beat slower when you are at rest, which saves wear and tear on your heart muscle. Ultimately, your walks will strengthen your heart and increase its pumping efficiency, improving your overall aerobic status. Also, think about your body as a container of fluids. You have blood, lymph, and other fluids that just more or less pool when you are inactive. It may be that your ankles swell when you sit for too long. Getting out and engaging in physical activity moves those fluids around and shakes things up for the good. Think of a mixed drink that requires a good shaking to make the perfect beverage.

In regard to load-bearing benefits, your body must carry weight when you stand and uses a variety of muscles, bones, tendons, and ligaments. Walking strengthens these structural components and lets them know that they are in demand and to be prepared for more physical activity. Inactive behavior is defined basically as remaining still, whether lying or sitting. Especially in older individuals, and especially older women, being inactive not only decreases muscle mass and weakens your skeletal system, but it also leads to bone loss (osteopenia and osteoporosis) in key areas such as your hips and spine. It's not uncommon for an elderly person to break a hip as a result of this bone loss. In fact, it is often the case that the hip breaks, causing a fall, versus falling and causing a break.

According to Braun and colleagues, inactive behavior is a significant predictor of bone loss at the femoral neck [26]. The femoral neck is located at the top of your femur, where the ball of the femur joins the socket of the hip and is a common site of breakage in older persons, especially women. Braun's team notes that "According to the International Osteoporosis Foundation, it is estimated that one in three women over the age of 50 years will sustain an osteoporosis-related fracture" [26]. So, it's very important to interrupt periods of inactivity, even if just for a few minutes, and engage in an activity that tells your bones to keep absorbing calcium to remain as strong as possible. And, it's never too early or too late to address sedentary behavior. Your dog is highly dependent on you as well, as the same mechanisms of inactive behavior affect him as well as you. While osteoporosis is not seen as much in dogs, it does occur.

The Centers for Disease Control and Prevention (CDC) support strongly the positive relationship between physical activity and overall health. According to the CDC: "Regular physical activity can reduce your risk of developing type 2 diabetes and metabolic syndrome. Metabolic syndrome is a condition in which you have some combination of too much fat around the waist, high blood pressure, low HDL cholesterol, high triglycerides, or high blood sugar. Research shows that lower rates of these conditions are seen with 120 to 150 minutes (2 hours to 2 hours and 30 minutes) a week of at least moderate-intensity aerobic activity. And the more physical activity you do, the lower your risk will be." [11]

Not only will physical activity reduce the occurrence or severity of diabetes and metabolic syndrome, but "Being physically active lowers your risk for two types of cancer: colon and breast" [11]. Findings also suggest that physical activity lowers the risk for endometrial and lung cancer as well. Another important aspect is that physical activity can reduce the effects of arthritis and other joint conditions. What's really exciting is that "People who are physically active for about 7 hours a week have a 40 percent lower risk of dying early than those who are active for less than 30 minutes a week" [11]. That's huge. Work up to walking your dog for thirty minutes twice a day and live significantly longer and healthier.

MANAGING DEPRESSION THROUGH PHYSICAL ACTIVITY

As you know, your dog is a source of joy and the more quality time you spend with her, the stronger that bond will become. But it may be that you live with depression, which makes it harder for you to stay healthy and be well. Statistics say that you are not alone. According to the World Health Organization, more than 300 million people of all ages suffer from depression [27]. Also, "Depression is the leading cause of disability worldwide, and is a major contributor to the overall global burden of disease" [27].

What is depression? Is it just sadness, not being happy? According to the Pew Research Center, "Just a third (34 percent) of adults in this country say they're very happy…Another half say they are pretty happy and 15 percent consider themselves not too happy" [28]. It's my professional opinion that these numbers apply to pet owners as well. William Styron makes it clear in his memoir *Darkness Visible* that depression is insufferable, a serious malady. "…[A] sense of self-hatred…" he calls it. "…a general feeling of worthlessness…dark joylessness…a failure of self esteem…" [29]. One would do most anything to escape it. Styron also said of his own condition that a "…failure of alleviation is one of the most distressing factors of the disorder…" [29]. Depression is a debilitating illness and being active with your dog may help decrease some of that suffering. Depression, like hypertension, is not curable with a magic pill, but involves treatment of the whole body, and that's where being active with your dog comes into play. There are even dogs who take medications for depression such as Prozac, and veterinary behaviorists attribute depression in some dogs to a lack of physical activity and loneliness experienced while their owner is away. On a positive note, the CDC has good news regarding physical activity and mental health: "Not only can regular physical activity help keep your thinking, learning, and judgment skills sharp as you age. It can also reduce your risk of depression and may help you sleep better. Research has shown that doing aerobic or a mix of aerobic and muscle-strengthening activities 3 to 5 times a week for 30 to 60 minutes can give you these mental health benefits." [11]

Thus, you may be depressed, and there is no shame here, but it's up to you to sort out those activities and perhaps professional help that will create that sense of wellness in both you and your dog. You deserve it, and so does your dog. Now, let's hear about Rosey.

ROSEY'S STORY

Morbid obesity in humans is generally defined as being one hundred pounds overweight for your height or having a body mass index, which is a ratio of height to weight, of forty or more. Being morbidly obese could also mean that you're already suffering from obesity-related medical disorders such as diabetes, high blood pressure, and/or heart disease. Most likely, if you are morbidly obese you will have trouble sleeping due to sleep apnea and will have trouble walking due to painful joints. It's a tough place to be, and many turn to surgery as a last resort.

It's pretty much the same scenario for a morbidly obese dog, except it takes less weight gain in a dog to be morbidly obese. I have seen some really heavy dogs in my practice, but none perhaps top a Rottweiler named Rosey that I met just a few years ago. We normally think of Rottweiler's as big and husky. They look tough and are often protectors of the family. A Rottweiler can be an imposing creature but in the right hands can also be a beautiful pet. Well, let me say that there was nothing imposing about Rosey. She could barely breathe. Rottweilers can tip the scales at 110 pounds, which is a big dog, but Rosey weighed in at 141 pounds, dangerously overweight for her frame.

To get Rosey out of the car, we used a sling to help lift and ease her to the ground. The only way she walked into the clinic was with a person on either side helping to support her weight with the sling. I could only think how miserable Rosey must feel. Not surprisingly, and as often is the case, her owners appeared to suffer from obesity as well. It's to their credit, though, that they finally did realize that there was a problem and that Rosey needed help and quick.

As part of her veterinary examination, it was discovered that she had an enlarged heart and was in the first stages of congestive heart failure. Basically, the enlarged heart does not pump efficiently, allowing blood to back up in the veins, which causes tissue swelling and forces fluid into the lungs. Untreated, Rosey could have died within perhaps days or at the most weeks. The owners were of course devastated to hear this, not realizing just how sick Rosey was. But, we got their attention and put Rosey on a very aggressive plan to reduce her weight and increase her physical activity. Basically, this entailed low-fat dog food fed twice a day and no snacks other than raw vegetables. For physical activity, we asked that the owners construct a sling at home using an old blanket and walk her outside to the street and back, twice a day, just to begin. That was only about one hundred feet total, but Rosey was in such bad shape that we couldn't push too hard.

We wanted to do a follow-up in seven days, but it was two

weeks before the owners could return with Rosey. To be honest, I have been disappointed many times when owners do not or cannot follow through with recommendations, so I was braced to find Rosey in even worse shape. Eagerly I watched the clock, knowing that Rosey was scheduled at eleven. I fully expected to have to use the sling again and was stunned to see Rosey wobble in under her own power. She was still slow and breathing noisily, but I could tell right away that a corner had been turned. The first thing I did was congratulate the owners, knowing that they had taken Rosey's best interest to heart. They were beaming with pride, and so was I.

Once again, we thoroughly checked her out. Her blood pressure had dropped as well as her respiratory rate, although she was still in bad shape, but so much improved. A year later, Rosey was still a bit overweight, but had lost a total of twenty-four pounds, which is really astounding. Her breathing was normal. She could sustain twenty-minute walks, and the swelling and coughing were gone. And, her owners looked better as well. It's hard to think healthy just about your dog. Often those good instincts wash over from the pet to the owners, as happened in Rosey's case.

THE SCIENCE BEHIND PHYSICAL ACTIVITY IN DOGS

Exercise physiology is the study of the effects of exercise and training on normal functions of the body. Understanding what's normal in humans allows us to understand the responses to exercise in dogs and allows us to maximize the effectiveness of a conditioning program. This includes not only physical benefits but mental benefits as well. As we have noted, inactive behavior is associated with an elevated risk for developing dementia and Alzheimer's Disease [20]. So, there are plenty of good reasons to engage in physical activity, not just to lose weight but to engage in what Ernie calls "life enhancement."

MUSCLE PHYSIOLOGY

As in our own bodies, there are three types of muscle in the dog's body: cardiac (heart), smooth (intestines), and skeletal (muscles). Skeletal muscle plays a large role in exercise and physical performance. It is important to understand skeletal muscle structure and function in order to understand the effects exercise has on it. Most muscles contain thousands of muscle fibers that span the entire length of the muscle, cross at least one joint, and are composed of different fiber types.

Skeletal muscle fiber types are classified based on how they contract and how they use energy. Generally speaking, muscle fibers are considered to be either slow twitch or fast twitch. Slow-twitch fibers are well suited to perform aerobic activities such as walking and resist fatigue. Fast-twitch fibers are good for activities such as sprinting and are capable of generating higher levels of force but are less resistant to fatigue than slow-twitch fibers.

Muscle fibers can be classified in various ways and based on this some "change" can occur. As an example, with endurance training, as the oxygen capacities of fibers are improved, fibers can "shift" into another category. Thus, prolonged endurance exercise can promote a shift of fast-twitch muscle fibers toward slow-twitch. Other changes associated with long-term endurance training typically include an increase in blood supply to the muscles, which increases the delivery of oxygen and nutrients to the muscle. Whether much fiber type change occurs or not, endurance training is beneficial for the overall health of dogs and improved physical function.

Muscle energy comes from food, and dogs and people use

their sources of energy (carbohydrates, fats, and proteins) very differently. In general, humans rely much more on carbohydrates and much less on fat. When we run low on blood sugar we become tired and the body may switch to burning fat for calories. Dogs are able to use fat for energy much better than humans and save their carbohydrate stores.

Fatigue occurs when the contraction of skeletal muscle cannot continue indefinitely. There are several explanations for the cause of fatigue. One thought is that fatigue can originate from psychological factors that may enhance or limit performance. The drive to run and play, generated by your enthusiasm, might allow some dogs to continue to participate in physical activity despite tiredness, simply as the result of verbal encouragement, whereas other species would not continue regardless of the praise.

CONDITIONING AND TRAINING OF SKELETAL MUSCLE

Conditioning of skeletal muscle involves performing exercise that prepares the muscle for the specific task that it will be asked to perform. Training is usually geared toward the type of sporting event or activity the dog will be involved in. During exercise training, athletes are frequently pushed until unable to continue. This is commonly termed the overload principle, which refers to the need for a system to be exercised to a level beyond that which it is accustomed for training to have an additional effect. This principle applies to the cardiovascular system, the musculoskeletal system, and other body systems. Factors that influence overload include intensity, duration, and frequency of a particular exercise. The harder you exercise on a regular basis, the harder it will be to reach fatigue.

Most types of exercise training can be divided into either endurance or strength-training activities. It's important that training uses the systems and structures involved in the activity. For example, a dog that pulls sleds would be better served to run while pulling something as opposed to trotting for a long duration on a treadmill. In humans, engaging in training activities that target specific muscle group's results in muscle change. For example, endurance exercises, such as running long distances, increases the capacity to produce energy by improving blood flow and metabolism. High levels of endurance are very important in dogs that participate in prolonged periods of exercise such as sporting, herding, and long-distance racing dogs. Endurance relates to the ability of a muscle or group of muscles to undergo many repetitions under low loads or to continue an exercise or activity over long periods. Endurance exercise usually targets specific muscle groups involved in the specific activity and lasts for a prolonged time, usually greater than fifteen minutes. Endurance exercises for dogs include trotting, running, swimming, land and underwater treadmill activity, and long-distance sled pulling. This is a far cry from the simple walks with your dog that you will start with but shows how far you and your dog can eventually go.

Muscle strength is associated with an increase in muscle size. Fast-twitch muscle fibers produce more force and contract at a higher velocity than slow-twitch fibers. Strength training increases the size of fast-twitch fibers more than slow-twitch fibers. The enlargement of muscles that happens with strength training occurs as a result of growth of muscle fibers and not adding muscle fibers. When you walk with your dog, the leg muscles will grow stronger. Strength in dogs is mainly related to speed and the ability to carry or pull loads. Strength is also important for dogs that must accelerate and decelerate very rapidly, such as dogs that participate in agility competitions. Genetic factors also play a role. Sprinting breeds, such as greyhounds, have a greater percentage of fast-twitch muscle fibers, whereas breeds such as foxhounds have larger percentages of slow-twitch fibers. Regardless, your regular walks with your dog will cause your and your dog's muscles to develop and perform better.

Next is Jasmine's story.

JASMINE'S STORY

Often, it's the case that society seems to throw away certain persons, whether it be for a disability or some disorder that makes them less useful than "normal" people. Jasmine was such a person who felt that the world had tossed her aside. She was in her mid-thirties and suffered from multiple sclerosis (MS), a debilitating disorder of the muscles. She lived alone in an apartment, which did not allow pets, and tended to stay in her wheelchair all day, even though she could walk short distances.

Jasmine, who was officially disabled, had a social worker who suggested that she get out of the apartment and do some volunteer work. It took about six months for that to sink in, all while she just sat brooding and feeling useless, but she managed to show up one day at the animal shelter. It was no small effort, as she had to take the bus. At first, we weren't sure about how well Jasmine would be able to navigate the shelter, which is made of different buildings. Although she was determined, she seemed afraid to ask for help of any sort.

I could tell that Jasmine was really getting into loving those homeless dogs, and cats too. She would make her way down the cement hallway, as the dogs barked ferociously, and carefully open the gate and wheel herself in, the wheelchair barely fitting. At first, she would spend half an hour in a single kennel cage but soon learned to use her time to visit with as many dogs as possible.

Jasmine admitted that she had almost given up hope, and that the dogs had given a new meaning to her life. We soon learned that Jasmine was perfect to work with therapy dogs and she began to get involved with their training. She was so patient and fell in love with all of the dogs, but especially Trinnie, a five-year-old Lab mix with scruffy ears. Jasmine could not have animals in her apartment, but claimed Trinnie as her dog, and you would think that Trinnie was her best friend, and it was true.

Ultimately, working with the dogs encouraged Jasmine to eventually venture into the kennels without the safety of her wheelchair. Although she was not overweight, working with the dogs increased her mobility, and encouraged her to walk more, which was a joy to see. You could just see the sparkle in her eyes as she would lead Trinnie into the fenced yard. It just goes to show that with dogs, giving a little earns a lot in return.

INJURIES TO WATCH OUT FOR

When we are active, there are risks of physical injury. It may be that you or your dog already lives with arthritis. Arthritis is an inflammation of the joints that can be aggravated by physical activity, in both dogs and humans. Should you or your dog suffer from arthritis, you should take precautions to minimize further injury. As always, consult with a health professional if you find that arthritic joints, or other conditions, interfere with your ability to walk and engage in physical activity.

In dogs, all four limbs are of direct concern as weight is distributed between them. Large breeds such as Labradors are often diagnosed with hip arthritis. It may be that you have arthritis of the fingers, which will make it difficult for you to handle a leash. In that case it may be that you do better with a retractable leash that has a solid handle to grip. If your arthritis is mild, you can probably get by with over-the-counter drugs such as aspirin or ibuprofen, but you should always consult with a physician just to make sure that the treatment matches the problem.

If you notice that your dog's walking is off or that he is limping, this could be a sign of various injuries that need to be examined by your veterinarian. In humans and dogs, it is not uncommon to tear a ligament, most commonly the anterior cruciate ligament (ACL), or cranial cruciate ligament (CCL) as it is called in dogs, which is located in the knee. In people, ACL tears result from extreme stress on the joint, but it is usually a degenerative process in dogs. Both people and dogs go through rehabilitation after surgical repair for this.

A less common disorder seen more in dogs than humans is displacement or luxation of the kneecap (or patella). Luxation occurs when the kneecap slides out of place due to a twisting force or due to misalignment of the bones. Following surgery, the soft tissues must be allowed to heal. Icing and use of anti-inflammatory drugs are used to decrease swelling and reduce pain. Initial activity should be limited to short leash walks.

Spinal disk injuries are not uncommon in dogs. This is particularly true for dogs with long backs such as Dachshunds and Corgis. Obesity is a significant contributing factor to disk injuries. If you suspect a disk injury or have a dog with a sagging back who has difficulty walking, you should visit your veterinarian for advice. But, as a general rule, regular physical activity and proper feeding to reduce weight are always necessary.

There are a variety of other physical injuries that respond well to weight reduction, including muscular imbalances, chronic pain, arthritis, and overuse injuries. As noted by Ernie, who is the founder of the Association for Pet Obesity Prevention, 54 percent of dogs in the United States are obese or overweight. Chances are good that your dog is overweight and that he is vulnerable to injury. So, to prevent and minimize injury, it's important to know what your dog's caloric needs are versus overfeeding. As you have learned from Ernie, paying close attention to what and how much your dog eats is critical to getting healthy with your pet. It may be that you say, "He's always been a big boy," or you may describe your dog as "husky" or "chunky," but most likely this is just code for "fat." But, take heart that good nutrition and physical activity can turn your and your dog's life around and help prevent and heal physical injuries.

BASIC PRINCIPLES OF STRETCHING

So, let's go a little more in depth on stretching. *The American College of Sports Medicine's Guidelines for Exercise Testing and Prescription* recommends (for people) that each exercise session start with a warm-up, followed by the physical activity such as walking, then a cool-down, of which stretching is a part. Stretching, which can be performed either after the warm-up or cool-down (or both) should take place for several minutes. Although these guidelines are for humans, many of the same principles apply to dogs as well.

After a dog has warmed up, specific stretches geared toward the type of activity that will be performed or that address tightness or problem areas in the dog may be performed. According to the American College of Sports Medicine (ACSM), "Flexibility exercise is most effective when the muscle is warm. Try light aerobic activity or even a hot bath to warm the muscles before stretching" [30]. Common areas for stretching include: hips, shoulders, neck, and back muscles.

If a dog has sustained an injury that has resulted in tightness, such as in an Achilles tendon injury, careful stretching of the tight area may reduce a recurrence of the injury. Strengthening exercises combined with stretching may provide the best long-term protection against re-injury. To stretch a muscle, yours and your dog's, it should be put in a position that produces a slight pull on the muscle but not to the point of pain. While there are books and resources on stretching your dog you may need to find a veterinarian or canine therapist to help teach you this. A list of canine rehab and fitness professionals can be found here: www.utvetce.com/find-a-pro. According to the ACSM, the position in which a slight stretch is felt should be held for ten to thirty seconds "to the point of tightness or slight discomfort" [30]. You should repeat each stretch "two to four times, accumulating 60 seconds per stretch" [30]. The stretch position should not cause pain or take the joint past the normal range of motion. Stretching increases a joint's range of motion [31]. This means that with effective stretching you will notice more flexibility overall in your joints and muscles.

For a simple look at various stretches, visit the National Institute of Health's Go4Life website at go4life.nia.nih.gov/exercises/flexibility.

ACSM guidelines recommend that stretching activities be done at least two days per week, but you can stretch before each walk on a daily basis. If some joint motion is limited or stiffness occurs, range of motion or stretching activities should be done daily. Here are some general stretching principles:

Slowly put the joint in a position that produces a slight pull on the muscle but not to the point of pain.

Stretches should be held fifteen to thirty seconds, and each stretch should be repeated four to ten times on each side of the body.

Stretch at least two days per week. If some joint motion is limited or stiffness occurs, range of motion or stretching activities should be done daily.

Two areas you should focus on stretching include the hip

and shoulder. Be careful, though, stretching too vigorously prior to warming up may cause injury. It is logical to follow a general approach to warm-up and cool-down exercises without being "dogmatic" about exact rules. Just stretch while it feels good to you and your dog. You do not want to introduce pain. Warming up your dog can include walking for a few minutes followed by gentle manual stretching of forelimbs and hind limbs. You may find that you do not have the time to stretch yourself and your dog before each outing but try and include stretching in your and your dog's routine at least twice a week. Now, let's hear about Sam.

SAM'S STORY

Sam was a big beefy guy who looked a bit like Teddy Kennedy, tipping the scales at over 300 pounds. An engineer by profession, his job kept him in a chair and in front of a computer most of the day. When he was fifty, he had his first heart attack, really lost ground with his overall health, and was kept from physical activity by serious arthritis and inactive habits he had picked up as a desk worker.

Needless to say, he was a mess when he first came to my clinic for outpatient rehabilitation. We worked together, slow and steady, until he could walk comfortably for twenty minutes without assistance. He was desperate to get back to work and within a month his wish was granted.

As I got to know Sam during his rehabilitation, I discovered that he had two beautiful golden Labrador retrievers. Naturally, I inquired about the health of his dogs and his response didn't surprise me. The dogs lived indoors, were never walked, and were "big boys" according to Sam. We talked about combining his therapy with walks with his dogs, and he was very receptive to the idea, eager to ward off another heart attack and genuinely concerned for his dogs.

He started off with twenty-minute walks, noticing that his poor labs were as winded as he was. Within three months he was up to forty-five-minute walks, twice a day, and was shedding weight along with his beloved pets, and that was ten years ago. Now Sam has a new dog, a long-haired Sheltie, and I often see him out and about, slimmer these days and with a smile on his rugged face.

The lesson is that it's never too late to get active, especially with your dog. Sam did have another mild heart attack, but without his increase in activity with his dogs, the outcome could have been much worse.

RUNNING RACES WITH YOUR DOG

Whether it's the Iron Dog, the Mutt Strut, or just a dog-friendly race, many dog owners are taking their dogs along for the run. Many breeds of dogs can easily outrun a human. For example, Brian Duff and his Weimaraner Kaydom set the world record for the dog-human mile in 2006 at a blistering four minutes and thirteen seconds. After the race, Duff noted that he was actually holding Kaydom back. "I was just trying to run as fast as I could to keep up with him," Duff said [32].

There are several breeds of dogs that make good runners. There are the obvious breeds such as greyhounds that often race for a living and huskies that are noted for sled pulling. Pit bulls, though, are also known as good running partners. You might even be surprised to learn that Jack Russells make good running buddies. The best way to find out if your dog likes to run is to give it a try. Breeds that are not very good runners include pugs and bulldogs who may do more snorting and overheating than running.

As always, start off slow, walking at first to give your pet the chance to condition. It could be the case that you need to condition your heart and muscles as well. Once you and your dog are comfortable with thirty-minute walks, try a ten-minute run in the cooler part of the day. Running necessarily puts more stress on joints and muscles, so be alert to any weaknesses that you or your dog may have and watch for signs of injury such as limping.

Owners often ask me if their dogs need some kind of foot protection, especially if the walks are long or if they are running with their dog. It's common for long-distance hikers who hike with their dogs over rugged terrain to have their dogs wear protective footwear. In general, though, the pads on a dog's foot are tough and durable. Do be aware, though, that walking your dog on hot pavement can lead to injuries. If you walk or run with your dog in hot weather, choose lighter-colored sidewalks versus blacktop surfaces that are much hotter. A benefit to running and walking is that the dog's nails naturally wear down, saving you the trouble of trimming.

One thing to consider about running races, such as a 5K or a 10K, with your dog is that it sets a very definite goal. It's another way to break out of the routine and provide motivation for those daily walks. Plus, you get a t-shirt! And, just because it's a race doesn't mean that you have to run. There will always be those who choose to walk so you'll have some company. You can also choose to alternate between running and walking, setting a pace that feels good to you and your dog.

One consideration, which we have discussed, is to realize that humans and dogs have two types of muscle fibers, slow-twitch and fast-twitch, which perform different functions. Slow-twitch fibers are good for endurance, and fast-twitch fibers are good for sprinting. There are some exercises that you can do with your dog to promote both kinds of fibers. To develop slow-twitch fibers the simplest approach is to do long walks with your dog. To strengthen fast-twitch fibers, you want to create greater force on the legs. Sprinting with your dog is ideal, if your dog is up for it. Once you and your dog can take sustained walks, add in some fast walking or jogging. Just remember, a healthy dog is an aerobic machine and will most likely be able to outlast you.

Next, we have Derek and Angel.

DEREK AND ANGEL'S STORY

Living in Boulder, Colorado, must be tough if you are not fit. Boulder is known for its population of runners, bikers, hikers, and skiers. It's one of those fit towns where there is a lot of outdoor activity. Derek lived in a suburb of Boulder, was thirteen years old, and had brown hair and freckles. His mom said that he'd always been overweight and even used the word "lazy" to describe him, although she whispered when she said it. At the age of eleven, Derek weighed 155 pounds. At his height, he should have weighed about 90 pounds, defining him as obese for his height and weight.

When asked about what his favorite foods were, he surprised me by saying broccoli and ice cream. It turned out, though, that he loved deep-fried broccoli that he dipped in ranch dressing, which may have even more empty calories than ice cream. Derek was an only child and his parents had always doted on him, spoiling him as they admitted. And one of the ways they spoiled him was by letting him eat whatever he wanted whenever he wanted, including a lot of fast food.

When Derek was eleven, his parents surprised him with a dog for his birthday, a feisty beagle puppy about six months old. Derek was overjoyed and loved playing with Angel after school. He saved his allowance to buy her a special bed for his bedroom, and much to his parents' surprise began taking Angel on short walks around the neighborhood. Another surprise was that Derek insisted that his parents only buy "good dog food" from the pet store and not food from the grocery store. He even picked out the brand, having done his own research on the Internet. His parents were astounded.

A year passed, and Derek's weight did not decrease but it also did not increase, and he looked fitter and was much more active. His dog walks stretched out to thirty minutes, sometimes forty, and he then began to do short jogs with Angel, who loped along, ears flopping and nails tapping the sidewalk. In talking with Derek's parents, it was apparent that Derek had somehow taken control of his destiny and set forth on a path to general fitness. After Angel came along, he too began eating healthier, going so far as to eat salad on occasion. His parents caught on, and they made an effort to decrease the amount of fast food coming into the household. And so, as Angel had inspired Derek, he began to inspire his parents to be more fit.

Needless to say, all of Derek's attention to Angel resulted in a healthy dog who could do a 30-minute jog with ease. A year ago, Derek took his physical activity with Angel up a notch and asked his parents to register him for a local canine 5K race. By this time, he had actually begun to lose weight, just a few pounds, but at a time when growing rapidly, so he actually began to slim down. The race was dog friendly and drew hundreds of participants from Boulder and beyond.

To prepare, Derek saved his money to buy Angel a special harness and leash, and his parents pitched in for a sleek pair of Brooks running shoes. Three weeks prior to the race in April, Derek began taking Angel out for short runs in the morning as well as after school. He still huffed and puffed and worried that he wouldn't be able to finish the race, which began to loom large in his mind.

When race day rolled around, Derek was shaking with excitement. Angel wouldn't eat that morning, and so Derek decided he would skip breakfast as well, but he drank two glasses of orange juice, and prepped his water bottle, which he would carry while he ran. It had been a cold night, dipping down to freezing, and the day broke still very chilly. Once at the race site along the Boulder Reservoir, surrounded by people and dogs, Derek felt that he might faint, and Angel barked her beagle woof, which made her sound like she had a sore throat. At one point, Derek's dad had to take Derek aside and have him take slow deep breaths.

"Pop!" and the race was on. Derek and Angel trotted at first in the crowd of people, which soon thinned. With his heart beating a mile a minute, Derek and Angel hit their stride. Angel could actually run faster than Derek and sort of pulled him along, although he was distracted by the other dogs, sometimes slowing to check them out. Derek ran his heart out and finished with a time of thirty minutes and twenty seconds, which is pretty good for a thirteen-year-old boy and his dog.

DOGS AND CHILDREN

As with Derek, it's widely recognized that there is an obesity epidemic in the United States. According to the CDC, 36.5 percent of adult Americans are obese [33]. Consequences of obesity include hypertension, type II diabetes, stroke, cancer, and other disorders. It's not only adults who are obese. It's estimated that up to 20 percent of children and adolescents are obese [34]. The costs of obesity are staggering, most recently estimated at $147 billion [33]. Couple that with 56 percent of dogs being overweight or obese, and it looks like there is plenty of opportunity for dogs and humans to engage in physical activity.

However, a child with obesity does not necessarily have to

engage in physical activity with an obese dog. A healthy dog will do just fine and might even provide more motivation for children combating obesity. In general, studies show that people who own dogs are happier than those who don't. And, interestingly, 93 percent of people who currently own pets grew up owning pets, 40 percent of those pets being dogs [35]. Pets are family in more ways than one.

Dogs are a source of comfort, according to psychologist Lance Workman [35]. There is just something about having a dog in the household that creates good vibes, as silly as that may sound, but kids especially know it to be true. Here is some good news from Pets at Home:

"Pets at Home's research discovered that keeping a pet increases your chances of happiness during childhood—particularly if you choose a dog. Of the 2,438 respondents who had owned both a cat and a dog, 65 per cent claimed that dogs had brought them most happiness overall, and 54 per cent believed that dogs had brought them most happiness as a child." [35]

Not only does the child have the benefit and joy of that dog-human bond and an early sense of responsibility for another living thing, he or she is generally happier and prone to be more physically active than a child without a dog. It's never too early for a child to begin to learn how to care for a pet, although the average age is between seven and eight.

We're especially interested here in the health benefits of pets and there is good news, also from the Pets at Home report. "[O]wning a pet could lead to a variety of physical health benefits for children, including lowering the risk of childhood obesity and improving allergies" [35], which is great news. But remember, this applies to adults as well.

The formula is pretty simple. If you own a dog, you are more physically active. Of course, just owning a dog is no guarantee of health benefits. You have to walk and play with the dog, who is always willing given that he is in good health. In the United Kingdom it has been estimated that pet owners lost a total of 56 million pounds within 12 months due to the health effects of owning a pet [35]. You can think of your dog as your best friend and also as a personal trainer. Veterinarian Deborah Linder agrees: "Pets may be able to offer motivation and unconditional support that will help children stay committed to their weight reduction goals" [36].

WORKING OUT WITH AN OLDER DOG

So, you have an older dog and perhaps wonder what the limitations of age may bring in terms of physical activity, which is a good instinct. In general, you can consider your dog an older dog, or geriatric, according to these general rules.

Dog Size	Dog Weight	Dog Age
Small dogs	(0-20 lb)	11.48 ± 1.86 years
Medium dogs	(21-50 lb)	10.19 ± 1.56 years
Large dogs	(51-90 lb)	8.85 ± 1.38 years
Giant dogs	(> 90 lb)	7.46 ± 1.27 years

It's pretty obvious that heavier dogs age more quickly, and they will need the most consideration when playing, running, or walking. Let's take a look at what the effects of ageing are on an older dog, which I divide into metabolic effects and physical effects. Most importantly, obese animals have shorter lifespans than non-obese animals.

One's metabolism is generally unique but subject to a wide variety of factors including genetics, diet, physical activity, and immune status. An older dog, like an older human, will have a decreased metabolic rate, making the dog move slower and store calories as fat versus burning or converting calories into muscle. As Ernie would tell you, an older dog with a lowered metabolic rate needs to eat less, but still needs to eat healthy. Engaging the dog to run and play will force the older body's tendency toward sluggishness into activity, signaling the older body to essentially "wake up and smell the roses!" By working out with an older dog you stimulate her to better health, improving the ability to fight off infections and autoimmune disorders such as rheumatic arthritis.

The physical effects of ageing are numerous. The percentage of body weight made of fat increases, which stresses the heart and contributes to obesity. The heart as it ages becomes less efficient and is often compromised by a build-up of plaque in its arteries. Cardiac output decreases, which is basically the amount of blood being pumped out by the heart within a minute. Working out with your dog helps to stabilize and improve cardiac output, making each beat of the heart an efficient one. Closely related to the ageing heart are the ageing lungs, which lose elasticity over time, decreasing the efficiency of each breath taken. Physical activity combats this process, increasing the amounts of oxygen and carbon dioxide exchanged per breath.

Ageing is very noticeable in a dog's skin, muscles, and bones. Skin becomes thickened, hyperpigmented, and less elastic. Footpads become thick and hard, and claws become brittle. Muscle, bone, and cartilage mass are lost, and arthritis becomes more common with ageing. All of these conditions can be helped with physical activity, which works magic with the older and ailing body.

Also interesting to note, are factors that affect a dog's lifespan. I've already mentioned obesity. Smaller dogs will almost always outlive larger dogs. Mixed-breed dogs also have a longer life expectancy than purebreds, which makes adopting dogs from local shelters, which tend to be mixed breeds, more of a positive idea. Dogs that are "fixed," neutered and spayed, tend to live longer. And finally, dogs that live inside have longer lifespans than dogs who live outside.

Given these considerations, how do you maintain the quality of life of an older dog? As always, before you begin a physical activity routine, you should take your dog to a vet for a physical, especially if the dog is older. There are any number of common disorders such as bone disease or hypothyroidism that may require medical intervention before physical activity is started, although the exercise will benefit most disorders by forcing the body to overcome characteristics of ageing.

In general, support programs should be implemented as part of a wellness screening for animals eight years and older. This will allow the veterinarian to target geriatric-related health problems and to detect geriatric disease early enough to implement effective medical care and offer preventive healthcare measures. You, the dog owner, play a large role in this process. You should be instructed on the normal process of ageing, nutrition, and appropriate exercise to understand your dog's overall quality of life.

Exercise in the ageing dog should be performed to tolerance. Don't push too hard. Low-impact exercise, such as swimming, or frequent leash walks should be implemented on a consistent, daily basis. Arthritic humans participating in controlled, low-impact exercises have improved function, reduced pain, and need less medication, which translates overall to your dog as well. Using legs that may ache is actually good for the joints and cartilage, as long as there is not disease or injury present. One key to physical activity is the notion of weight-bearing. Just the act of standing and moving helps protect joints and organ systems. Mild weight-bearing exercise also helps stimulate cartilage and increases nutrients to your body.

You may worry that your dog is in pain when walking or

playing. A dog with arthritis will necessarily be slower and stiffer, but physical activity will limber the joints and sometimes relieve the pain. If a dog favors a leg or winces (yelps) when walking or playing, definitely see your veterinarian before doing any damage. Your vet may recommend anti-inflammatory medications. There are other treatments for pain that you can implement at home. The first is the use of hot and cold packs for sore and aching muscles and joints. Inquire with your vet as to the best method of using these. The second method of pain reduction is massage. We all know how a good massage feels. Massaging increases blood flow to the area and loosens tight muscles. Some other methods involve treatments such as laser and TENS units, which are relatively new with dogs. Your vet will need to prescribe this, and it is typically done in their office.

What are some environmental considerations for the geriatric dog? A young puppy might enjoy the brisk outdoor air of a backyard, but an older dog needs some protection from cold and damp environments. Your dog should be moved from a cold, damp, outdoor environment to a warm, dry, inside environment. A soft, well-padded bed should be provided. You can go the extra mile by using a circulating warm-water blanket under the pads to provide heat, which may reduce morning stiffness. This may seem like a lot, but your ageing best friend deserves it.

One key is to maintain a balanced physical activity routine. You may be tempted on a weekend to possibly overdo it and stress your older dog unnecessarily. Climbing steps is great for a younger dog but can be difficult with an older dog. Ramps are a good solution, especially if you too are ageing or are affected by conditions such as arthritis. Again, physical activity in the ageing dog should be performed to tolerance. Don't push him too hard. Dogs, whether young or old, are pretty good about letting you know they are tired. If you're on a walk and your friend just sits or lies down or is panting, then it's time for a break.

Next is a story from a client named Heather, told in her own words.

HEATHER'S AND LOUANN'S STORY

I met Dr. David after my dog Louann developed asthma. She's a dusty-colored mix with some Lab and would wheeze even when lying down. I had taken Louann to the vet, and he recommended that I see Dr. David to help with Louann's weight. To be honest I needed help with my own weight as well. At the time, Louann weighed a whopping 119 pounds. I knew that Louann ate too much, but I always felt guilty if there was no food in her bowl. I would just refill it every time she emptied it, which I now know is the wrong approach. Plus, I gave her snacks, usually table scraps.

When the vet told me that Louann was morbidly obese, I asked him if that meant she was fat. She did look like a fat sausage. When he said that she was "super fat," it kind of hurt my feelings, but I felt bad for letting her get that way. Over the years she just got lazier and lazier to the point where she would just eat, go back to her doggie bed, and lay down and snore. When she walked through the house, she snorted and I could tell that it was hard for her to breathe. That's when I took her to the vet, not really thinking that her weight was to blame.

The first thing the vet had me do was to cut back on the food and give Louann a diet dog food. When I told the vet that I sometimes bought her a hamburger at Burger King, he frowned. But because she was in such bad shape, he also had me make an appointment to see Dr. David about some exercise counseling. By now I was really worried that they thought I was fat too. But, of course, I was!

Dr. David was very nice and avoided the word "fat." He checked Louann and said that we would have to work slow and get her back in shape. He made sure that I was following the vet's advice on feeding her and recommended that we start with an underwater treadmill. Louann was so big that her weight was stressing her legs and hips. I thought that was an odd thing to do, especially for a dog, but I was committed to doing the right thing for Louann. At twelve years of age, she was practically my daughter, my only son Travis having moved out a few years before. My husband died when Travis was only ten, an accident at a pipe mill.

To get her ready, I gave Louann a bath, which nearly killed her and me, lifting her into the bathtub. She was definitely a big girl. And getting Louann into my pickup truck was another chore. She just couldn't get in, and didn't want to get in, not even for a treat. I finally just gave her the treat and did my best to drag her onto the floorboard. She was panting and had a crazy look in her eyes, like she was saying, "What are you doing to me?"

At the facility, which had a shallow pool, a nice young man helped get Louann out of the truck, and she waddled in, huffing and puffing. I felt so bad, like I was a bad mother. Dr. David was there and with the help of a young woman got Louann into the pool and onto the underwater treadmill. Poor Louann! She looked so afraid. At first, she wouldn't walk and just rode the treadmill backwards, but with some coaxing by Dr. David, she gradually got the hang of it and walked ever so slowly. About every three minutes, Dr. David stopped the treadmill to let her rest and catch her breath. I just had no idea how out of shape she was, and me too.

For a month, three times a week, I took Louann in for her treadmill sessions, and she did better each time. After we would get home, she would lumber to her bed and sleep for an hour, like she was exhausted, and I guess she was. The next step was walking outside, just ten minutes at a slow pace to start. I could tell already that she was improving, although she was still stiff and sometimes limped just a bit. After three months of walking, we were doing thirty minutes at a time, and after about eight months total, we were walking for thirty minutes twice a day. And the result? Well, we both lost weight. It may not seem like much, but Louann lost twenty pounds, and I lost fifteen. We were both eating better and exercising. Louann still has a touch of asthma, but she doesn't sleep as much, and she gobbles up carrot pieces that I give her as treats. Overall, Louann is healthier, more active, more alert, and she has inspired me to take better care of myself.

AN ACTIVE LIFESTYLE FOR BETTER HEALTH

I hope that the information and inspirational stories provided here give you the hope and courage that you need to live a healthier and more active lifestyle. It does take willpower and thought, but you now have the tools you need to make it happen for you and your dog. Remember that the first seven days of physical activity are all about starting slow and building toward bigger goals. Next, Tricia, Ernie, and I have some tips on how to build a social support system around yourself that will help you to achieve happiness with your best friend.

WEEK FOUR: BUILDING COMMUNITY

—Montgomery, Ward, and Levine—

There are so many reasons that having like-minded individuals around you is important. You are reaching for a better you, a better dog, and a better life and need that social support that holds you accountable for your dreams and pursuits. You can even think of it as love, the love that you need to make your goals known and accepted by others, to be encouraged by others. Strength comes from within, but others provide the extra support that you need. And let's not forget the dog with whom you are entering into this pact of better health. Think of your people friends and your dog as family who are cheering you on.

HEALTHY SOCIAL NETWORKS

According to Dr. Robert Kushner, "…one pattern that's clearly emerged among people who succeed is the presence of social support. If you have a doctor, a neighbor, a spouse, a friend, or a support group backing you up, cheering you on, and helping to keep you honest, you have a better chance of success than if you go it alone" [18].

How does this work? Social support reduces stress, which in turn reduces the effect of diseases such as high blood pressure [37]. In one study, nervous system "reactivity to brief psychological stress was lower when a friend was present than in the alone condition" [37]. Your nervous system operates in the background and controls such bodily processes as heart rate, breathing, and digestion, and it responds to the positive energy of social support, whether it be a friend or a trainer. Having a social support system can even improve your immune system.

So, what is it about having friends and family who support you? Researchers note that what is often at work is self-regulating behavior. When you go out to eat alone, you are more likely to buy or eat unhealthy foods, especially if you are making an effort to eat better. Having that companion with you helps to overcome negative behaviors and enhances self-regulatory behaviors that result in buying and eating healthier foods [38].

It is also true that the quality of your social support is a consideration. Just having a spouse or a lot friends in your social network does not necessarily mean that you have the social support that you need [39]. You need to have that friend or relative or professional who knows what your goals are and the challenges that you face to meet those goals. Ideally, there are already others close to you who understand, but that is not always the case. You need to seek out those who will support you unconditionally. Luckily, you can count on your dog for unconditional support as well as love. So, take heart that you are starting off at a good place. Don't dwell on what you don't have and focus on what you do have.

Having that social support system can make you healthier and even help you to live longer. According to researchers Park, Yu, and Lee, "Positive social interactions have…been shown to exert powerful beneficial effects on health outcomes and longevity" [40]. Having that supportive neighbor, friend, trainer, rehab clinician, or relative will not only make you feel better, and feel better about yourself, but will have "a positively significant influence on mental fitness" [40]. Think about it. It is so worth it to put some time and energy into surrounding yourself with caring people who want you to succeed. You deserve it, and your dog deserves it as well. If you are shy or have trouble meeting new people, think about your dog and draw encouragement from him or her.

Ultimately, your dog is your best partner so do not fret if your social network is thin at the beginning. Becker and Kushner note from their research that a dog is capable of providing emotional support much as a person is [18]. According to them, "A four-legged workout partner…is one who will never, ever let you down—not even when 'forgetting' about your workout is exactly what you'd like to do" [18].

WORKING WITH A TRAINER

Initially, during this first month, it may be just you and your dog, and that's okay. The two of you together can do amazing things. Perhaps you are shy about discussing your fitness plans with others. That's okay, too. Everyone is different. But, having that extra encouragement from others will make your journey that much easier. Seeking a trainer may not be your cup of tea, but you should consider all options that broaden your community of support.

The fundamental principles and advice given in this book stem from our knowledge and experience of building communities for owners to get healthy with their dogs. A trainer can provide the tools, the motivation, the training, and the family needed for any dog owner to succeed in improving the quality of their and their dog's life.

A trainer will be a friend who suspends judgment and works toward the better health of you and your dog. Ultimately, it's the focus on the dog that helps to take away harmful judging behaviors. There's no better non-judgmental companion than your dog. In addition to judgment, another thing that is lacking with a trainer is competition. The only competition is with yourself and with your dog, not with others. You measure progress according to your own goals and success alongside the trainer. Smiles replace egos when your best interest is at stake, as you and your dog lose weight and build strength, agility, and endurance. That's a beautiful thing.

In regard to building trust, we know that those who work with you have to earn your trust. They get to know you and put themselves in your shoes. One important aspect of beginning your journey to a better you, better dog, better life is a thorough evaluation of you and your dog. A trainer wants to know the details. Whether you are a janitor, stay-at-home mom, or busy professional, a good trainer asks the right questions and gets good answers. You learn to trust your trainer, realizing that they want to help you be your best. They want *for* you versus wanting *from* you. It's not about how much money you make or what your background is, but it's about feeling good in your life, knowing that you are doing the best for you and your dog. A good trainer keeps up with you, checks in on you. "How are you feeling? You mentioned your hip. How is it going?" Trainers have to have the helper's attitude, that gift to inspire and coach without judgment and without making the journey a competition but a mutual endeavor between you and your dog that rests on trust.

Whether with a trainer or just with your dog on your own block, you'll find that this trust comes primarily through your dog. Emotions run up and down the leash. You may have suffered emotionally, perhaps having just been through a divorce or the death of a loved one. Some dog owners are so thoroughly beaten down by life that the first training session may actually be without the dog. This builds confidence. It's important to want to come back and not just be thrown into the mix.

You have to feel good about your prospects of doing well

or you may not build that first level of confidence. And then, as you begin to lose weight and learn new skills with your dog, the confidence increases and spurs energy. Easing into your trainer's program is easier if you are ready and the trainers are adept at facilitating that. You will find that you want to do this not only for yourself, but for your dog as well. You can lose weight, become more fit, and have fun at the same time.

There is no pressure to hire a trainer. It may be too expensive or just not your thing. It's likely that a trainer does not exist in your town. But, as you progress in your journey, give it some thought and consider seeking out professionals who understand your journey to a better life with your dog.

EXTENDING YOUR FAMILY

With a trainer, it's not just about the classes. There is also the social element. You'll find that you bond with the trainer and perhaps with other dog owners. It's not just about working out and having fun in the classes but having fun in life as well. It's common for trainer's clients to hook up for walks with their dogs. On these walks, clients become friends, become each other's biggest cheerleader. Knowing that not only you and your dog are losing weight, but others as well, builds confidence and fosters an accountability to reach your goals.

One important component of a good trainer is to instill inspiration, which ultimately comes from within. Trainers can recognize that inspiration, that desire to reach just a little bit higher, and focus that inspiration back onto you. Inspiration also comes from watching others and their dogs. You'll think, "Oh, she can do that move and so can I!" Trainers are very careful to keep the focus on you, to build that inspiration as self-sustaining. It's best if you do not become dependent on a trainer, though. When that trainer goes away so too may your inspiration. Trainers encourage you to look deeper into yourself to feel uplifted in the privacy of your own home and on walks alone with your dog and also provide a social network.

Both in the classroom and outside the classroom, members get excited about helping themselves and helping others. When they are able to do a move and the dog does it too, there is that moment of joy. Perhaps you are working a stability ball and your dog, after trying a few times, is able to hold a position. You think, "My dog did that" and "I can to." There is an excitement you can feel, which builds confidence that with encouragement from the trainers is inspiring to both dog and you. You help your dog, and she helps you.

And it's never about being pushed. Whether in a class, nutrition counseling session, or rehab activity, professionals never push anyone but allow them to push themselves. With therapists and trainers, the proper term is encouragement. "You got this! You can do this!" You successfully finish a basic course, and you're ready for more, feeling confident and inspired, going at your own pace. Although the therapists are key, it's you and your dog who are the epitome of enthusiasm and encouragement.

It's just that love for people and dogs and a passion for what you do. Trainers cannot just be a dog lover. They have to love people as well. Trainers strive to help the dog and you and are always seeking ways to better themselves with the goal of a better you, a better dog, a better life.

Ultimately, we realize that you are not just floating in the air, an isolated case to be fixed. You are part of a community and always building that community, keeping in mind your personal goals and aspirations, which is community in the truest sense. Getting fit is not about six-pack abs but about quality of life. Everyone is welcome regardless of size, gender, skin color, or religion. The dogs are the beautiful bond that brings everyone together to seek the best for each other. A supportive community knows no bounds.

Now, let's listen to Marissa's story.

MARISSA'S STORY

Marissa, a former high-school cheerleader, had always been ten to twenty pounds overweight, especially since having two daughters. Working at the department of motor vehicles in her home town of Lansing, Michigan, Marissa was on her feet most of the day, but always had a big lunch to help her make it through the day and always wound up feeling stuffed and guilty.

When her oldest daughter headed off to college, there was a void in the house, and she adopted an ageing collie mix from the local shelter. The dog's name was Mamie, and Marissa decided to keep the name. Surprisingly, Mamie was overweight by fifteen pounds. Mamie didn't have a waist and Marissa couldn't feel the dog's backbone through the layer of fat there. When she would let Mamie out in the backyard, inevitably she would just relax under a large maple tree.

At the age of forty-three, Marissa began to notice that her hips and knees, especially her left knee, were becoming stiff. When her husband, an occupational therapist, suggested that losing five pounds would take away a significant amount of strain on her joints, she was shocked that he would say such a thing. Needless to say, her husband was in the dog house for a few days, but at a routine check-up with her physician, she asked if what he had said was true, and it was!

One morning she happened to be watching the *Today Show* on NBC and saw a segment that featured Tricia demonstrating how easy it is for dogs and people to work out together. This got Marissa thinking, and made her determined to get Mamie and herself back into shape. She didn't have a gym she could go to and decided to begin regular walks with Mamie, at first just in the mornings for twenty minutes and then after work.

It happened to be winter, with lots of snow on the ground, so she bundled up and soon found that her twenty-minute walks in the brisk air were not enough. She settled into a routine of thirty-minute walks and by spring had lost six pounds. Mamie had also lost weight, the layers of fat on her body thinning to show the muscles beneath. Marissa had worried that the walking would aggravate her sore joints, but just as her husband and doctor had predicted, the soreness diminished, and she felt much more comfortable on her long days at work. By summer, she had lost a total of eleven pounds and the pains had completely subsided. When her daughter returned from college, she noticed the change in her mom right away.

Marissa's only goal was to lose those five pounds, but with the support of her husband and physician, she was able to double that and keep off the weight. She now weighs 135 pounds and says that she feels great not only for herself but for Mamie as well. She also notes that Mamie seems to be better behaved, barking less at strangers, and that she stopped trying to dig holes beneath the backyard fence.

DOGGONE HEALTHY

Having a support system to deal with life's challenges is so very important. The same applies when you are seeking to increase the quality of your life through nutrition and exercise. This fourth week of your journey is the place to begin thinking about that wider of community of like-minded people and pets who can help you and your dog get the best out of life.

Dr. Ernie realized later in his career, as he writes in Week Two, that enhancing life for you and your pet is not only an issue of simple nutrition but that there is a physical and behavioral aspect as well. He developed a program devoted to weight loss, nutritional counseling, and physical, behavioral, and social training in a facility called Doggone Healthy. In an indoor and outdoor environment, complete with treadmills, trainers, and classes, Doggone Healthy brought out the best in pets.

Dr. Ernie remembers vividly a classic case, Bo, a middle-aged chocolate Lab. Over the past several years, Bo had been gaining weight. His semi-retired owners still worked every day and had little time for Bo's physical needs. What Bo really needed was not only exercise but also community. Of course, the owner felt guilty, but did the right thing and brought Bo in for an assessment.

Based on his temperament, Bo was placed in a class with six other likeminded dogs. Bo loved the feeling of being with a pack, running with his new friends. Bo was a dog looking for an opportunity to thrive. He was a smart dog and you could see the competitive side of him emerge when he was with his new peers. While teaching new skills such as stair stepping, Bo was watching the other dogs, seeming to say out loud, "Hey, I can do that better!"

Bo lost weight with no diet change and became more active at home. His owners said, "Wow, he's sleeping better and has more spring in his step." Bo's life was being enhanced. The next step was nutritional counseling to guide Bo into losing another seven to eight pounds, using simple dietary interventions. Dr. Ernie focused on what he calls "power calories" from higher protein foods and a switch to vegetables for treats. The better nutrition combined with the socializing and physical activity of doggie day school changed Bo's life. You could tell he was happier, more alert, and enjoying life. He began developing muscles, replacing rolls of flab, and looking long and lean. Bo's owners were really proud of his progress.

Dogs love to run with a pack and owners love to hear from a trainer, "Hey, Bo really crushed it today. He can really can weave and bob." These activities and accomplishments inspire both dog and owner. It's a great feeling to be able to provide your dog with opportunities to learn and grow, and dogs thrive at being the best they can be. When quality of life is increased, for both humans and dogs, we respond—and want more! We are happier, feel better, sleep better, and are more emotionally stable and fulfilled.

BUILDING TRUST AND COMMUNITY

Dr. David works with patients in nursing homes, long-term-care facilities, and rehab hospitals, primarily with the elderly, often incorporating dogs into the wellness program. At veterinary clinics, he works with dogs in need of rehabilitation and weight loss. He knows that any time you or your dog are striving to be healthier that having emotional support from an extended community of helpers is vital. Being in the presence of others with the same needs and who have had similar experiences is one of the best motivations to keep on track and push yourself to better health.

Regarding his clients, people and dogs, David first gets to know them to build friendship. He is not there to force his advice on the dog or owner, but to first make them comfortable using positive reinforcement. For dogs and owners, this would involve the imparting of a few encouraging words. It works similarly with dogs. It's a matter of being open, listening, and watching. People and pets always appreciate encouragement and have that need to be heard and feel that one's needs are being met.

Seeking help through rehab or a trainer to lose weight and be more fit comes with a built-in community that is supportive. There is a great deal of positivity that comes from an extended community of helpers. They are there to look at the big picture, to see how they can facilitate the best in you and your dog. They are your cheerleaders, committed to motivate you and keep you positive. The enthusiasm trickles down to the individual. People lift each other up, breaking down walls to better health.

Confidence is a key component of community building. Many people at first may feel uncomfortable in a gym or rehab center. The trainers and therapists, though, are there to identify your struggle and give a hand. A new person in a class or therapy session may feel like an outsider at first, but you are made to feel a part of the group. Building confidence within your dog is also a goal. This is especially true of shelter dogs that may have trust issues. The trainer is there to make sure they get plenty of attention and provide activities at which they can succeed, while giving praise. The timid dog, having experienced success and praise, will respond, much as a human. Often you can almost hear your dog say, "I can't wait to get outside!"

David notes that the most common problem to overcome is a defeatist attitude. You may not think that you can do a particular exercise, but the trainers are there to encourage you and help you along at your own pace. It's important that the trainers get to know the individual and read them for the little signs that they are ready to go to the next level. Although motivated for different reasons, everybody likes positive reinforcement. By the time you commit to therapy or a class, you are already motivated and primed for success. There is no judgment. One's progress is not measured by what others can do, but by what you and your dog feel comfortable with.

And so, in the hands of trainers, therapists, or a dog-walking friend, the idea is to thrive. You have to let that trained professional or trusted friend guide you. They are going to provide you with enthusiasm, passion, respect, and confidence, all toward the goal of making you and your dog more fit and healthy. Trainers, especially, understand what the vision is and are there to be empowering as well as be genuine. You'll find that you begin to hold yourself accountable to others in the group and the trainers or therapists. It's a neat thing when other people are watching you succeed. It enhances your need to be better and improves and boosts your confidence.

Next, we have a surprising story.

TOD'S STORY

Tod was a long-haul truck driver who lived alone, having divorced. His three sons were all in college, and he worked overtime to pay for their education. Sitting for hours in a truck can result in a number of physical ailments including weight gain, back pain, stiffness, muscle weakness, and can even lead to life-threatening blood clots in the legs, for which he had been hospitalized once.

Feeling terrible about his health and feeling slow and sluggish, one day at a highway rest stop he noticed several people walking their dogs. He says it was like a bolt of lightning from the sky. He'd heard of other truck drivers who traveled with a dog, but he'd thought they were just a little crazy.

On a day off, he visited the local shelter in his hometown of Charlotte, North Carolina, and picked out the chunkiest dog there, a black-and-white bulldog he named Stumpy because of his short legs. Like a good dad, he bought Stumpy a bed that he placed in the seat next to him and bought a black collar with silver studs on it, giving Stumpy the look of a gangster.

It took some getting used to, for both him and Stumpy, but soon Tod found himself stopping more often and taking fifteen-minute walks with his new friend. He found that having

Stumpy along for the ride decreased his coffee and junk-food intake, and he felt like he had a friend with him on those long hauls. He even thought that Stumpy made him a more careful and diligent driver.

Within a month, Tod had lost a few pounds (he never weighed himself, but his pants began to sag), and he could tell that Stumpy was losing weight too. He soon discovered through talking with fellow truckers that what he was doing was not that unusual after all. Many truckers have taken the same path, building companionship and physical activity with help from a faithful canine friend.

LET YOUR DOG OPEN THE DOOR

It goes without saying that dogs make great companions, reducing stress and giving us an excuse to get fit. It may be that you are unsure about getting out in your neighborhood, whether for safety reasons or perhaps you just feel uncomfortable. Having a dog with you gives you that excuse you need to make your fitness goals real. No one is likely to say, "Look at that oddball walking his dog." In fact, they are more likely to trust you and perhaps give you a hearty "Good morning!"

Dogs serve many purposes in our social networks. There are dogs trained to warn their owners who have epilepsy when a seizure is coming on. Nursing homes often have a day when a therapy dog will visit, giving love to all who need it. But most of all, dogs make great companions, having lived with humans for tens of thousands of years. You might even say that we need one another.

So, let your dog open up the opportunity to expand your social and support network. This next story shows just how beneficial a dog can be in bringing people together.

BECCA'S STORY

Becca was a single woman, twenty-three years old, and overweight since childhood. She remembers her eating problems developing after her sister drowned in a terrible accident. She was devastated, and like many of us do turned to food to drown her sorrows. She graduated from high school weighing over two hundred pounds and particularly liked to eat fast food.

In college, she added an additional twenty pounds and graduated with her nursing degree. She felt badly that she was slower than the other nurses and often felt out of breath while hurrying down the hall to give medications or respond to a call light. After work, she would hit the drive-thru of her favorite hamburger place and begin eating even before she got home.

Lonely in her two-bedroom apartment, Becca decided that she needed a friend. She'd always wanted a poodle and visited a local pet store on a Saturday, where shelter dogs were being adopted, and there was a poodle, larger than she had ever seen before, with a dull, white, curly coat. The dog's name was Maxi, and Becca couldn't take her eyes off of her, but left the pet store feeling overwhelmed.

The next day she went back and much to her surprise, Maxi was still there. Without hesitating she filled out the paperwork and paid the $75 adoption fee, buying some dog food, a collar, and a brush. With Maxi in the car, shaking as if with a newborn baby, Becca wondered what she'd gotten herself into.

Living in an apartment complex, she'd never felt comfortable walking around, but soon Becca found herself out on fifteen-minute walks with Maxi. That's when she met Ellen, an older woman who lived in the same building. Maxi opened up an opportunity for them to talk and Becca learned that Ellen used to walk around the entire complex, but that she felt she was now too old to walk alone. On a whim, Becca asked if Ellen would like to walk with them, and Ellen broke into a huge smile, nearly crying.

It took a few days for them to mesh their schedules, but soon Becca, Ellen, and Maxi were doing the full loop around the large complex, about half a mile, talking the whole time. Within a month, they were doing two loops and even venturing onto the sidewalk that led down into the center of town.

Naturally, they encountered others who were walking their dogs and Becca got to know even more people in the complex, and she was losing pounds and almost back down to her high school weight. She was ecstatic, feeling better and feeling less lonely as well in the company of her new friends, Maxi and Ellen. But the story does not stop there.

About six months into their long walks in the morning and afternoon, they began to encounter Rick and his ageing German shepherd, Noble. At first, Noble and Maxi growled at each other, but soon began to accept one another's presence. And suddenly, to Becca's amazement, she and Ellen were walking with Rick and Noble. Becca really began to focus on her nutrition and within eight months was down to 175 pounds, which she considered a minor miracle. Rick became a permanent part of their walking group, giving Becca two new friends who supported her and who made her feel much better about herself.

YOUR DOG AS SOCIAL SUPPORT

As evidenced by Becca's story, dogs can serve as a "social connector," increasing the chances of social interaction and having chance conversations with complete strangers who may become friends [3]. If you have ever been to a dog park, you know how easy it is to strike up a conversation with a stranger because they think your dog is cute or that your dog seems to like their dog. It may seem too simple or even silly, but it's true.

According to Zeltzman and Johnson, "You can build upon the love you share with your dog to reach a greater goal: to lose weight or stay fit" [41]. So, it may seem to some like a chore to work on your social support network, but just keep the goal in mind.

Often, one's community of support may be expanded because of illness or injury. According to researchers, "The use of therapy dogs has a positive effect on patients' pain level and satisfaction with hospital stay after total joint replacement" [42]. Having the therapy dogs present during therapy made the patients happier, improved their pain, and resulted in a more satisfying hospital stay. So, if you suffer from an illness or injury, look into adding a dog to your life. It may be that you do not need to lose weight, but the dog will provide encouragement and could possibly help with your healing process as well as your social network.

You may also think of your dog as a therapeutic friend and companion. According to Deborah Wells, "As well as providing a source of companionship, support, and, entertainment, there is now substantial evidence to suggest that such animals may be able to promote their owners' health…" [3]. Wells notes that the idea of pets as being beneficial to humans is not new and proving it scientifically gives truth to the idea. Something as simple as petting your dog has been shown to decrease blood pressure and reduce heart rate, and it also soothes the pet. As Dr. Ernie would note, it's better to give your dog praise and a good belly rub instead of a junk-food treat.

Even just being in the same room with your dog reduces stress and provides "significant reductions in the frequency of minor physical ailments (e.g., headaches, colds, hay fever, dizziness)" [3]. These are short-term benefits, but the long-term benefits of interacting with a pet have also been shown, such as lowering the risk for heart disease. "The few studies that have been undertaken in this area seem to suggest that pets may hold long-term therapeutic benefits, preventing us from becoming ill, and even facilitating recovery from serious physical ailments" [3]. An interesting aside, Wells reveals that the stress of reading aloud by a child is reduced when a pet is present [3]. Who knew that dogs could help our children read better?

There is also a psychological benefit to owning a dog. Pets work wonders with emotions when going through stressful life events such as a death or divorce and can also reduce levels of anxiety, loneliness, and depression [3].

Don't like visiting the doctor? Wells says, "Pet owners… have been discovered to visit the doctor significantly less than individuals who do not own a companion animal" [3]. That alone should make owning a dog worthwhile. According to Uchino and colleagues, "…the associations between social support and physical health have been found on such diverse health outcomes (e.g., coronary heart disease, cancer, and infectious illnesses) that there are probably multiple physiological pathways by which social support may influence disease states." [37]

This is evident from research as well as through the stories of real people who have found in their dogs real friends and the motivation to live a healthier and happier life.

So, expanding your social support network, beginning with your dog, yields an abundance of positive health effects. There is a theory, called Attachment Theory, that seeks to explain why this is the case. According to the theory, we treat our dogs as members of the family, speaking to them like humans and confiding in them. Just as we build relationships with other people, we build relationships with our pets. Wells supports this through the research of Cobb who "described social support as information leading one to believe they are loved, esteemed, and belonging to a network of mutual obligation. In some respects, pets meet many components of this definition. For instance, they are typically perceived as nonjudgmental, noncritical, and to be there in times of trouble." [3]

This is so evident when you come home and your dog greets you, often going through a ritual of barking, whining, and generally just acting so grateful to see you. There is nothing like receiving the joy of a dog.

YOU CAN DO IT!

Having spent the first week getting motivated with Tricia, the second week working on healthy eating and feeding with Dr. Ernie, the third week learning how to be physically active with Dr. David, and the fourth week realizing the importance of social support from friends, neighbors, relatives, and professional trainers, you're ready to succeed and to begin a lifelong journey to wellness and happiness with your best friend, your dog. You will feel better, and your dog will to.

By taking care of yourself and your dog, eating healthy and taking walks, you are adding value to life. You are taking control and setting a goal to have a better you, a better dog, a better life. These first thirty days are key to your success, and we wish you the best. We wish you happiness with your best friend.

APPENDICES

APPENDIX ONE: TYPICAL FEEDING GUIDE

Adult Dog Size	Feeding Amount
3 to 12 pounds	½ to 1 cup
13 to 20 pounds	1 to 1½ cups
21 to 35 pounds	1½ to 1¼ cups
36 to 50 pounds	2¼ to 2¾ cups
51 to 75 pounds	2¾ to 3½ cups
76 to 100 pounds	3½ to 4¼ cups
over 100 pounds	4¼ cups plus ¼ cup for each additional 10 pounds

APPENDIX TWO: IDEAL WEIGHT RANGE BY BREED

Breed	Average Weight Range (lbs)
Afghan hounds	58–65
Airedale terriers	40–65
Akitas7	5–115
Alaskan malamutes	70–95
American Staffordshire terriers	55–65
Australian cattle dogs	30–35
Australian shepherds	40–65
Basenjis	20–25
Basset hounds	45–65
Beagles	18–30
Belgian Malinois	55–75
Bernese mountain dogs	85–110
Bichon frises	7–12
Bloodhounds	80–110
Border collies	27–45
Border terriers	11–15
Borzois	60–100
Boston terriers	10–25
Bouviers des Flandres	95–120
Boxers	50–75
Brittany spaniels3	0–40
Brussels griffons	6–12
Bull terriers Miniature	24–32
Bull terriers Standard	45–80
Bulldogs	40–50
Bullmastiffs	100–130
Cairn terriers	13–18
Cardigan Welsh corgis	25–30
Cavalier King Charles spaniels	10–18

Breed	Average Weight Range (lbs)
Chesapeake Bay retrievers	55–80
Chihuahuas	4–6
Chinese crested	Less than 10
Chinese Shar-Pei	45–60
Chow Chows	45–70
Cocker spaniels	23–28
Collies	50–70
Dachshunds Mini	8–10
Dachshunds Standard	10–12
Dalmatians	50–55
Doberman pinschers	65–90
English cocker spaniels	26–34
English setters	45–80
English springer spaniels	40–50
Flat-Coated retrievers	60–70
French bulldogs	19–22 & 22–28 (two standards)
German shepherds	75–95
German shorthaired pointers	45–70
German wirehaired pointers	60–70
Giant schnauzers	55–80
Golden retrievers	65–75
Gordon setters	45–80
Great Danes	110–180
Great Pyrenees	85–100
Greater Swiss mountain dogs	130–135
Havanese	7–12
Irish setters	55–75
Irish wolfhounds	90–150
Italian greyhounds	6–10 (two sizes: less than 8 or 8–10)
Japanese Chin	4–15 (two classes: under 7 and over 7)
Keeshond	35–45 and 55–65 (two standards)
Labrador retrievers	65–80

Breed	Average Weight Range (lbs)
Lhasa Apsos	13–15
Maltese	4–6
Mastiffs	150–160
Miniature pinschers	8–10
Miniature schnauzers	12–15 (2017 AKC: 11–20)
Newfoundlands	100–150
Norwegian elkhounds	40–60
Norwich terriers	10–12
Nova Scotia duck tolling retrievers	37–50
Old English sheepdogs	60–100
Papillons	7–10
Parson Russell terriers (Jack Russell terriers)	14–18
Pekingese Sleeve	less than 6
Pekingese Mini	6–8
Pekingese Standard	8–10
Pembroke Welsh corgis	23–27
Pomeranians	4–7
Poodles Mini	11–17
Poodles Standard	45–65
Portuguese water dogs	35–55
Pugs	13–18
Rhodesian ridgebacks	65–90
Rottweilers	70–135
Samoyeds	35–65
Schipperkes	12–18
Scottish terriers	18–21
Shetland sheepdogs	18–20
Shiba Inu	15–25
Shih Tzu	8–16
Siberian huskies	35–60
Silky terriers	8–11
Soft-Coated Wheaten terriers	30–45

Breed	Average Weight Range (lbs)
Saint Bernards	110–200
Staffordshire bull terriers	23–38
Standard schnauzers	30–45
Tibetan terriers	20–24 (18–30 based on conformation)
Toy fox terriers	4–7
Vizsla	45–60
Weimaraners	50–70
Welsh terriers	20–21
West Highland white terriers	13–21
Whippets	25–45
Wirehaired fox terriers	13–20
Yorkshire terriers	less than 7

APPENDIX THREE: PORTIONING YOUR DOG'S FOOD ACCORDING TO TARGET WEIGHT

Target Weight	kcals per day
5	138
6	152
7	165
8	179
9	193
10	206
11	220
12	234
13	247
14	261
15	275
16	288
17	302
18	315
19	329
20	343
21	356
22	370
23	384
24	397
25	411
26	425
27	438
28	452
29	465
30	479
31	493
32	506
33	520

Target Weight	kcals per day
34	534
35	547
36	561
37	575
38	588
39	602
40	615
41	629
42	643
43	656
44	670
45	684
46	697
47	711
48	725
49	738
50	752
51	765
52	779
53	793
54	806
55	820
56	834
57	847
58	861
59	875
60	888
62	915
64	943
66	970
68	997
70	1025

Target Weight	kcals per day
72	1052
74	1079
76	1106
78	1134
80	1161
85	1229
90	1297
95	1365
100	1434
105	1502
110	1570
115	1638
120	1706

APPENDIX FOUR: RECIPES FOR YOUR DOG

Salmon Rollovers
1 can (7oz) salmon
1/3 cup oat flour
1 tsp. parsley, minced

- Preheat oven to 350 degrees.
- In a medium-sized bowl, mix ingredients until well blended.
- Roll mixture into ½-inch balls and place on a greased or non-stick baking sheets.
- Bake 12-15 minutes. Let cool before serving.

10 calories per treat
yields 36 treats

Spring-in-Your Step Salad
1/8 cup parsley, chopped
¼ cup broccoli, chopped
¼ cup kale, chopped
1 kiwi, peeled and chopped
½ sweet potato, cooked and chopped

- Mix all ingredients and add 1/8 to ½ cup to your dog's regular meal

36 calories per serving, yields 3 servings

Super-Green Omega Bites
1 can (4.375 oz.) sardines packed in water
½ cup of oatmeal
2 tsp. spirulina powder

- Preheat oven to 350 degrees F.
- Using a food processor, grind oatmeal into a flour consistency and set aside.
- In a small bowl, mash sardines with water.
- Add the oatmeal and spirulina and mix well.
- Roll into small balls and flatten.
- Bake for 15 minutes, then turn off the oven and let sit for 10 minutes.
- Store in an airtight container or freeze.

32 calories per treat, yields 12 treats

Bee-Healthy Egg Scramble
½ tsp. coconut oil, extra virgin unrefined
1 egg, omega-3 enriched
1 tsp. raw local honey
¼ tsp. spirulina powder

- In a small skillet, heat coconut oil over low heat.
- Add egg and lightly scramble.
- Transfer egg to a separate bowl and add spirulina and honey.

133 calories

On Guard Winter Cookie
1 ½ cup water
1 1/3 cup Chickpea Flour
1 1/3 cup all-purpose Flour (gluten-free suggested)
1 cup Powdered Peanut Butter
½ cup dry Amaranth grain (optional)
1 cup ground Flax Seed
2 Tablespoon Turmeric Powder

1 Tablespoon Spirulina
2 Eggs

- Preheat oven to 350 degrees.
- Combine all dry ingredients in a large bowl.
- Add water and eggs and mix thoroughly.
- Turn dough onto a floured surface.
- Roll dough to ½ inch thick and cut out into shapes.
- Bake for 30 minutes.
- Cool before serving.
- Store in a sealed container.

100 bite-sized cookies, 24 calories each

Oh-Mega

2 –14 ½ oz cans or 3 ½ cups cooked salmon
1 cup cooked quinoa
1 cup chopped kale
½ cup chopped green beans
1 tbsp kelp powder
Makes approximately 6 cups

- Combine the kale and green beans in a blender or food processor and blend until minced or pureed.
- In a bowl, combine all ingredients and mix thoroughly. Divide into portions appropriate for your pet's caloric intake.
- Kale, spinach and broccoli should be avoided in dogs with kidney disease or certain types of bladder stones.

Tip

Quinoa (pronounced KEEN-wa), referred to as the mother of all grains, is a highly nutritious seed, and a good source of fiber and protein. It is easy to digest.

Quinoa should be rinsed thoroughly before cooking to remove all the bitter saponin coating (believe to be a natural insect repellent. Place the grain in a fine strainer and hold it under running water until the water runs clear. To cook, use two parts liquid to one part quinoa.

Turkey Pie
3 ½ cups cooked chopped turkey (light meat)
1 1/2 cup cooked millet
1 cup chopped raw broccoli
½ cup chopped apples
1 tbsp kelp powder
Totals 6 ½ cups

- Combine the broccoli and apples in a blender or food processor and blend until minced or pureed.
- In a bowl, combine all ingredients and mix thoroughly.
- Divide into portions appropriate for your pets' caloric intake.

Tip
Millet is a nutritious and low-allergen grain. Fresh fruits and vegetables are healthiest, but if you need to save time use frozen foods, not canned. Additionally, if your dog doesn't like raw veggies, try lightly steaming them instead.

REFERENCES

1. APOP, *Pet obesity grows in 2015*. 2016.

2. Lavie, C.J., P. Parto, and E. Archer, *Obesity, fitness, hypertension, and prognosis: Is physical activity the common denominator?* JAMA Internal Medicine, 2016. **176**(2): p. 217-8.

3. Wells, D.L., *The effects of animals on human health and well-being.* Journal of Social Issues, 2009. **65**(3): p. 523-543.

4. Holt-Lunstad, J., *Loneliness and social isolation as risk factors for mortality.* Perspectives on Psychological Science, 2015. **10**(2): p. 227-237.

5. Cuddy, B., *Is your dog depressed? Then look at your own behaviour*, in *The Gaurdian*. 2015.

6. Ogden, C.L., et al., *Prevalence of obesity among adults and youth: United States, 2011-2014.* NCHS Data Brief, 2015(219).

7. Helliwell, J., R. Layard, and J. Sachs *World happiness report 2016*. 2016. **1**.

8. Pratt, L.A. and D.J. Brody, *Depression in the U.S. household population, 2009-2012.* NCHS Data Brief, 2014(172).

9. German, A.J., et al., *Quality of life is reduced in obese dogs but improves after successful weight loss.* The Veterinary Journal, 2012. **192**(3): p. 428-434.

10. McConnell, A.R., et al., *Friends with benefits: On the positive consequences of pet ownership.* Journal of Personality and Social Psychology,, 2011. **10**(6): p. 1239-1252.

11. CDC *Physical activity and health: The benefits of physical activity*. 2015.

12. Kitahara, C.M., et al., *Association between class III obesity (BMI of 40–59 kg/m2) and mortality: A pooled analysis of 20 prospective studies.* PLoS Medicine, 2014.

13. Collaboration, *Body-mass index and cause-specific mortality in adults: Collaborative analyses of 57 prospective studies.* The Lancet. **373**(9669): p. 1083-1096.

14. Kealy, R.D., et al., *Effects of diet restriction on life span and age-related changes in dogs.* Journal of the American Veterinary Medical Association, 2002. **220**(9): p. 1315-1320.

15. Lawler, D.F., et al., *Influence of lifetime food restriction on causes, time, and predictors of death in dogs.* Journal of the American Veterinary Medical Association, 2005. **226**(2): p. 225-231.

16. Kane, E. *Boosting canine cognition.* DVM 360 Magazine, 2014.

17. Pan, Y., et al., *Dietary supplementation with medium-chain TAG has long-lasting cognition-enhancing effects in aged dogs.* British Journal of Nutrition, 2010. **103**: p. 1746-1754.

18. Becker, M., & Kushner, Robert, *Fitness unleashed.* 2006, New York: Three Rivers Press.

19. Pan, Y., et al., *Dietary supplementation with medium-chain TAG has long-lasting cognition-enhancing effects in-aged dogs.* British Journal of Nutrition, 2010. **103**(12): p. 1746-54.

20. Boecker, H. and A. Drzezga, *A perspective on the future role of brain pet imaging in exercise science.* Neuroimage, 2016. **131**: p. 73-80.

21. Stillwell, V. *Canine cognition.* n.d.

22. Stremming, S., *Getting real,* in *The cognitive canine.* 2017.

23. Hare, B., et al., *The domestication hypothesis for dogs' skills with human communication: A response to Udell et al. (2008) and Wynne et al. (2008).* Animal Behaviour, 2010. **79**: p. e1-e6.

24. Laughlin, S., et al., *Citizen science as a new tool in dog cognition research.* PLoS ONE, 2015. **10**(9): p. e0135176.

25. Leigh, P. *Fun, cognitive training games for dogs.* 2016.

26. Braun, S.I., et al., *Sedentary behavior, physical activity, and bone health in postmenopausal women.* Journal of Aging and Physical Activity, 2017. **25**(2): p. 173-181.

27. WHO *Depression.* Fact Sheet, 2017.

28. n.a. *Are we happy yet?* 2006.

29. Styron, W., *Darkness visible: A memoir of madness.* 1st ed. 1990, New York: Random House.

30. ACSM *ACSM issues new recommendations on quantity and quality of exercise.* 2017.

31. Page, P., *Current concepts in muscle stretching for exercise and rehabilitation.* International Journal of Sports Physical Therapy, 2012. **7**(1): p. 109-119.

32. Fox, K. *Dog-man duo sets new mile record.* Runner's World, 2016.

33. CDC *Adult obesity facts.* 2017.

34. Mitchell, N., et al., *Obesity: Overview of an epidemic.* The Psychiatric Clinics of North America, 2011. **34**(4): p. 717-732.

35. n.a., *The Pet Report.* 2015.

36. University, T. *Can dogs help kids lose weight?* News Release, 2014.

37. Uchino, B.N., Cacioppo, John T., & Kiecolt-Glaser, Janice K, *The relationship between social support and physiological processes: A review with emphasis on underlying mechanisms and implications for health.* Psychological Bulletin, 1996. **3**: p. 488-531.

38. Anderson, E.S., R.A. Winett, and J.R. Wojcik, *Self-regulation, self-efficacy, outcome expectations, and social support: Social cognitive theory and nutrition behavior.* Annals of Behavioral Medicine, 2007. **34**(3): p. 304-312.

39. Shinn, M., S. Lehmann, and N.W. Wong, *Social interaction and social support.* Journal of Social Issues, 1984. **40**(4): p. 55-76.

40. Park, W.R., et al., *1079 – Effects of psychological distress and social support on mental fitness among patients of mental health services.* European Psychiatry, 2013. **28**: p. 1.

41. Zeltzman, P. and R.A. Johnson, *Walk a hound, lose a pound.* 2011, West Lafayette, Indiana: Purdue University Press.

42. Harper, C.M., et al., *Can therapy dogs improve pain and satisfaction after total joint arthroplasty? A randomized controlled trial.* Clinical Orthopaedics and Related Research, 2015. **473**(1): p. 372-379.

www.ingramcontent.com/pod-product-compliance
Lightning Source LLC
Chambersburg PA
CBHW052056110526
44591CB00013B/2232